The Old Days

Letters from Theodore Shennan, 1940

Compiled by

CHRIS SHENNAN

THE CHOIR PRESS

First published in the United Kingdom in 2023 by

The Choir Press

ISBN 978-1-78963-354-2

Theodore Shennan

28 June 1924

Introduction

In 1940, Theodore Shennan wrote a long letter to his elder son, David. It was handwritten, in fountain pen, and was completed over a series of dates through 1940. It was begun on February 25th and then extended on February 29th, March 31st, April 18th, June 18th, and finally August 28th. There were apparently several other dates in between. By the time he had finished, the letter was 138 pages long.

The letter is essentially autobiographical and it describes 'The Old Days'. It includes Theodore's earliest memories in Bathgate, his childhood, his family, his medical training in Edinburgh and anecdotes about his medical colleagues in Edinburgh, Aberdeen and elsewhere. Theodore was born in 1869 and died in 1948. As such, his writing provides a record of the times through which he lived and about the people with whom he had contact.

The purpose of this publication is to make Theodore's letter more widely available as a record of family history and of the times through which he lived.

Chris Shennan (David Shennan's son)
November 2022

Theodore's Immediate Family

Parents

Alexander Shennan (1 August 1824 to 13 May 1891)
Jane Steele Lawson (23 March 1825 to 21 March 1914)

Siblings

John Shennan (7 March 1856 to 9 June 1939)
William Finlay Shennan (17 September 1857 to 5 April 1873)
Jeanie (Jean) Shennan (4 June 1859 to 19 March 1931)
Margaret (Maggie) Shennan (2 July 1861 to 31 January 1873)
Jessie Christina Alexandra Shennan (17 February 1863 to 20 May 1884)
Alexander (Lex) Shennan (20 January 1865 to (?) March 1952)
Lawson Storrow Shennan (10 August 1866 to 14 July 1936)
Isabella (Ella) Elizabeth Shennan (17 January 1868 to 6 May 1905)
Theodore Shennan (9 March 1869 to 21 October 1948)
      Married Minnie Green (Norwich) 30 July 1903

Children

Eileen Ivy Theodora Shennan (27 November 1904 to 12 May 1907)
David John George Shennan (8 March 1909 to 10 June 2001)
Edward Theodore Shennan (27 February 1916 to 5 October 1997)
Jean Lindsay Shennan (5 April 1936 to 1 September 2021)

Alexander and Jane's family, c. 1877.

From L to R: Jean, Lex, Ella, Alexander, Jane, John, Lawson, Theodore, Jessie.

3

Theodore's family, c. 1895.

From L to R: Lex, Lawson, Ella, Mother (Jane), Theodore, Jean.

Theodore's family, c. 1914.

From L to R: Minnie, David, Theodore.

25, Fonthill Terr.
Aberdeen.
26. 2 - 40

Dear David,

I am going to try & carry out my long
intended idea of giving you some description
of the old days; and for this you will need
to form some impression of the old home
where we passed so many eventful and
uneventful years. I am enclosing a rough
sketch plan of the old U.P. Manse at Bathgate.
It is of course from memory and cannot be
regarded as more than very approximately
correct as to detail & proportion. & comparative
size of the rooms.

The Manse at first stood separate from
the church; but some time before father went
there in 1865, from Houghton-le-Spring, Durham. a hall had been built between
them, and over it three good rooms added to
the house and at a higher level so that as
shown on 1ᵗ floor plan there was a short
flight of 5 steps in the upper passage. In
the old house there was no dampproof
layer in the walls, so that it was very damp
and, of course, unhealthy. Mother often
implored father to live in Edinburgh or some
other place more healthy for children; but
on £182 (at most) a year one could not do
much in that way: another result being of low salary
that he was well under the thumbs of his
session, a hard-headed & stubborn unfeeling
set of men for most part; though there were
pleasant exceptions

A year or so after they went there, at a

25 Fonthill Terrace
Aberdeen

26th February 1940

Dear David

I'm going to try to carry out my long intended idea of giving you some description of the old days: and for this you will need to form some impression of the old house where we passed so many eventful and uneventful years. I am enclosing a rough sketch plan of the old UP *(United Presbyterian)* manse at Bathgate.

It is, of course, from memory and cannot be regarded as more than very approximately correct as to detail and proportion and comparative size of the rooms.

The manse at first stood separate from the church, but some time before Father went there in 1867 (from Houghton-Ie-Spring, Durham), a hall had been built between them, and over it three good rooms added to the house and at higher level, so that as shown on the 1st floor plan there was a short damp proof layer in the walls, so it was very damp and, of course, unhealthy. Mother often implored Father to live in Edinburgh or some other place more healthy for children, but on £182 (at most) a year one could not do much in that way, another result being that he was well under the thumbs of his session, a hard-hearted and stubborn unfeeling set of men for the most part; though there were pleasant exceptions.

A year or so after they went there, at a spring cleaning, Mother found to her horror that mould was growing on the mattresses, but that was nothing to Chapman, the Session Clerk. He was a hard old stick.

Well, to return.

The dining room was a long low-ceilinged room which had been extended backwards after we went by taking in part of the coal house and scullery. A well-known minister, 6ft 4ins high, had to stoop going in at the door of it.

On the other side of the stone paved inner hall was what served as a parlour, and we had a doorway (without door) knocked through from it to the kitchen. Mother used regularly to clean the parlour vent by setting fire to it by lighting a newspaper in the grate. This was a bit risky as the rafters of the upper floor were not well isolated. However, she got off with it as a rule, the authorities being less particular then as they are nowadays. On the wall to the left of the wall opening – looking from the parlour – a big printed alphabet was stuck on the wall and it was said that I learned it off quickly by myself without help. Sounds a bit fabulous, but I had a perfect memory in those young days before school years, and could memorise a 5 or 6 verse hymn or psalm after one reading.

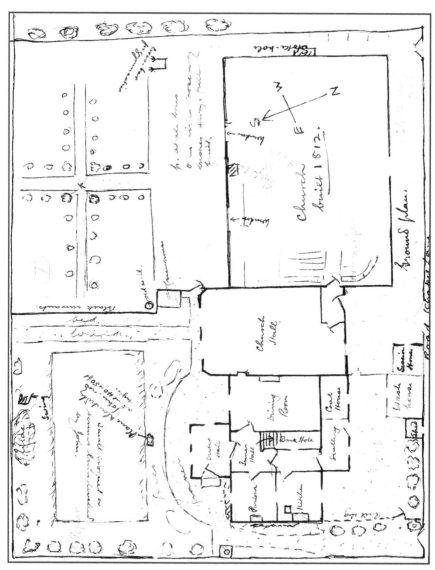

The Manse and UP Church at Bathgate.

The kitchen had a flagged floor and the range was cruel on coal, a whole scuttle at a time, but that did not trouble very much, as coal there was only 7/6 *(7 shillings 6 pence, 37 1/2 p)* a ton delivered from Balbardie pits a mile or two away. The small square near the range was a gas cooker on which I used to make cocoa in the early morning before doing lessons before breakfast. The cocoa making sometimes took up the whole time before it was time to take breakfast and bolt for the train to Edinburgh. That was when I was at the Royal High School from 13 to 16 years of age.

Outside at the front was a stone-flagged outer hall, with windows all round and shelves on which we managed to grow some plants and flowers and we used to climb up on the flat roof of this outer hall and so into the house by the bathroom window. We had many games making use of that flat roof.

We had some queer maids, and not too particular. I remember especially one we had when I could not have been more than 4 or 5. But it won't do to put it down in black and white, so remind me some time to tell you about it. It only shows how particular parents should be as to the character and precedents of girls, when there are young boys about.

On the gable wall (east) outside parlour and kitchen there was a big Jargonelle pear tree which sometimes had fruit on it. I could have produced good crops by pruning had I known then what I know about fruit trees now, and had had interest in them at that time. It has gone now and the gable is all cemented. The curly things are trees. The square on the wall opposite the parlour corner was an outside WC which let down to a drain which ran underground down along the east wall. Over a gravel walk was grass and John flatted a small area for very amateurish tennis and croquet, and in winter we flooded it for skating.

Along the south wall were other trees and especially a big old lilac tree on which we used to climb and which produced plentiful flowers in spring. Near it was a swing. Lawson was on it once, when I in a great temper threw a stone at him which caught his forehead and made a wound the scar of which he bore all his life. It was exactly the same spot in which I had to have one myself. I was going up Hopetoun Street to school and, as boys will do, was looking behind me. When I turned round I smacked right into a lamppost which cut through the skin. I had to go to a chemists near who put on some Vaseline. If I'm not mistaken, Ella had a scar at the same spot on her forehead.

Curious things happen.

The west wall between the flower (?) garden and the vegetable garden was recessed, for some unknown reason, near the house: and here John built the lean-to greenhouse which figures in my 'Orator Looks Back' and you'll note that it was just outside the windows of the church hall.

In the recess of this wall on the vegetable garden side was a covered in old well from which I expect the house drew water before pipes were put into the house. That was always a very serious thing to us youngsters, who, on lifting the stone covering the opening, could see the water still deep down.

Next to the church there was a stretch of grass – the clothes' green. I remember once watching John trying out an old smooth bored muzzle-loading fowling piece, there, on a target set against the church wall. The gun had been left in our charge by cousin Peter Shennan, brother of Hay who went out to Dunedin, New Zealand, in 1876. He was a working mason or builder, and we did not hear much of him thereafter.

The lower, larger part of the vegetable garden was divided by walks into four nearly equal squares. At the corners of these were apple trees, which, however, because of inexperience in pruning and so on, did not bear a great deal of fruit.

Along the walks on either side there were rows of gooseberry bushes of all kinds and all bearing good crops of fruit, eating and cooking. One year when I was alone or almost alone at home I thought it would be useful to pick all remaining gooseberries and make them into jam. Sugar was cheap, one and a half to two and a half pence a pound. So I got going but boiled and boiled the jam two or three times too long. The result was a solid mass in the huge jar, more like toffee than jam. I never heard the last of that effort; though the others did admit that when my jam was dug out and put into jam roly-poly, it was dashed good.

We used to work away in that garden and got quite a good amount of potatoes and cabbages out of it. The one and only time I played truant from school I thought I should redeem myself by going out and doing some digging: but Father's sharp eyes caught me and it being during school hours, I got well spanked for my pains in spite of my good (!!) intentions.

We once had a goat which gave very rich milk and it fed on that clothes green. The maid at that time – I would be 15 or 16 years old – was a huge, hulking country girl, rather soft. The goat was rather fond of her – she milked it – and it used to rub against her legs and butt her playfully. Her remark was 'Your kindness is nonsense, and absence is good company,' or something like that.

When a small kid, I used to trespass over the lower wall (south) over into old Mr Wardlaw's rhubarb field which was very naughty. Once I saw him coming up the field and beat it for the house, went up to the drawing room window and looked out as innocently as I could, but he saw me and shook his fist at me threatening all sorts of things. I got a fright that time.

To the west of the green, John put up two stout poles with an iron bar across the top which was used to do gymnastic exercises.

In the next garden – Mr Watson's – to the west was a row of tall trees just over the wall. These were splendid for climbing and often I went nearly to their tops, where I carved my initials. I expect they are there still.

The stoke hole for warming the church was to the west of it. The putting on of the fire on the Fridays was always an interesting operation.

You'll see that there was access right round church and manse; so that we and our friends had many races, and when at the High School I used to run round and round the passages in the church as a means of training: but I never made much of it: couldn't get up the speed needed.

Over the yard from the coal house was the separate wash house with copper and interesting rafters etc. etc. also good for climbing purposes.

Then a favourite ploy of mine was to climb up through a ceiling hole into the attics of the house, and thence through a roof opening with a removable cover on to the roof. Taking a rake with me I worked along the ridge, and down round the chimney head on to the part between the house and the church where there was a fine spot for lying in the sun. The risk never entered my head, and I did enjoy those ploys.

Every winter in those days there was heavy snow: and often the house was surrounded by 8 to 10 inches of snow through which we cheerfully tramped.

By the way, when I was a very small boy, John planted a plane tree just above next to the house – the croquet lawn. Last year I had a look at it and it is a huge tree, must be 40 or 50 feet in height.

Once when someone was cutting the grass, just about where I have written the word 'grass' he caught our fine curly haired retriever, Oscar, and cut deep into a leg. The poor beast bled a lot, but suitable treatment got him all right again.

Now I must get to the upper flat going up the curving staircase, down which I often and oftenfloated in my dreams without touching banister or steps.

At the top facing one is the door of the bathroom with a huge zinc bath supplied only with cold water. Still in summer the cold morning bath was the rule and enjoyed; and out of its window one got easily on to the leaded roof-flat of the porch. To the left, two bedrooms, occupied by the daughters of the house, and at one time the north room by a maid.

In the south room, marked 'spare room', was the birch bedstead which Lawson used till his death, and the larger mahogany chest of drawers which is now in your room. On the west side of the landing was the boys' room – Lex and Lawson – and at one time Father's study. The chest of drawers here was the bow-fronted one which stood on the upper landing at Downie Terrace. As an interfering youngster I thought I would clean it with soapy water and turpentine which, of course, took off all the fine polish. That was really a valuable piece which should have fetched a tall price at the sale as it had the original handles etc.

Next came the passage to the new part of the house, and up 5 steps to it. Opening from it, in the old part was the usual maid's room, a narrow crowded room, less roomy than indicated in the plan.

Then to the new rooms above the church hall, really the only good and dry rooms in the house. To the south, the large 'drawing room' which was Father and Mother's bedroom. The furniture that your Auntie Jean used was in that room and at the foot of the bed the old curved bow ended sofa, covered with plush which stood in the drawing room at Downie Terrace. I slept on it for years as a small kid, and on it I went through the awful night terrors from which active minded kids suffer. Every night for a long time I had a sort of low delirium before going to sleep which made me fear the approach of night. One night I had such a bad nightmare that the first waking thing I knew was flying down the five steps in the passage, yelling at the top of my voice, to be caught up by John who had rushed upstairs on hearing me, and got me just before I reached the stairs to the bottom flat. I must have had some chronic condition producing some evening temperature: but the experience was nerve-racking and I sometimes wonder that I kept my sanity. The bookcase along the east wall was a huge one: and two of its five sections are still downstairs in the old workroom.

Opposite the drawing room door was a smallish bedroom occupied by John when at home, and myself. There's a story I'll tell about that later, against myself.

The other room was Father's study, the two walls opposite the fire place and window covered

with large bookcases. Father had somewhere between 3000 and 5000 volumes, some fine old

leather-bound quartos.

The wardrobe in John's room was the (then) light coloured pine one that lately stood on the landing here where now the organ stands.

Well, the above will give you a sort of ground work of my early life and I'll tell you more in my next.

(End of first letter)

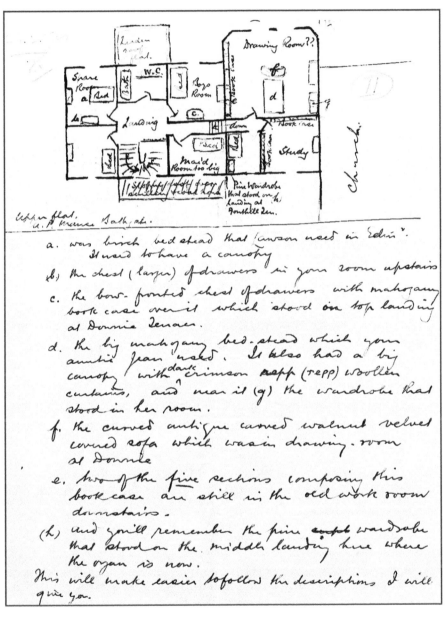

The upper flat at the Manse, UP Church, Bathgate.

15

29th February 1940

It is always very difficult to recall exactly and without doubt when one first appreciated the fact that one is a live and sentient being. I have two or three clear recollections, but the order of their occurrence is by no means clear.

For example, I remember distinctly lying beside Mother in her big bed, on the side next to the door with the clothes partly thrown back and Father on Mother's other side, with his arm thrown round her. I don't know if he was turning me or what, but Mother said 'Now, be careful, Alexander.' I can't have been more than two or three.

Then after my brother Willie's death I was lifted up by someone to see him lying in his coffin in the spare room surely an unconsidered action on that someone's part, to make that the one thing I remember about Willie. We had a rather smudgy photograph of him, apparently copied from a group of him, a thin delicate looking thin-faced boy, with a tailcoat and light coloured trousers. Fancy a rig-out like that for a boy of 15 1/2. Later poor Sandy had to wear these things at school, an awful ordeal, which must have accentuated his morbid shyness. When playing knifey on the grass patch in the Academy school-yard, he used to curl up his legs under him to hide the hideous contraptions.

Willie had begun work with Mr David Simpson in the Royal Bank branch in Hopetown Street. I think he had always been rather delicate and they used to tell me that he had some sort of abscess or breaking down gland on his cheek or upper part of his neck – no doubt tuberculosis.

This tubercle (consumption) infection appeared after going to Bathgate and I suppose we all had a touch of it, but whereas all four daughters died sooner or later of it, only Willie, of the sons, showed any evident effects. I sometimes have thought that my 'night terrors' from which I suffered so long could have been caused by some low grade tubercle infection – perhaps glandular, but one cannot tell. There may have been some predisposition from Father or Mother. Father had a scar on the side of his neck, possibly following glandular tubercle – like yours – but showed no other sign. I don't know much about Mother's folk except that her mother died at 35 or so; but from her almost rabid insistence that we all should be teetotallers, I think there was possibly an alcoholic element. One of her brothers was not very strong; but Father died at 66 of what was evidently a cerebral haemorrhage and Mother slipped away very peacefully within two days of entering her 90th year.

You'll get all the dates in the Register in the old family Bible, just before the New Testament.

I was just over 4 years old when Willie died on 5th April 1873.

I can remember absolutely nothing about my sister Maggie, who died on 31st January of the same year – the first break in the family: and curiously enough I cannot remember Mother or the sisters ever speaking much about her: she was 13 1/2 and died of tuberculosis, I believe. I'll ask Lex if he can remember anything about her.

There were still seven of us for another 11 years, with Father and Mother and a maid, i.e. 10 at least to be fed, housed and clothed on £182 a year, sometimes less but by that time John was beginning to earn a little and later he contributed something towards his own keep. They were happy years and of the week the Sundays, when all were at home, were the highlights.

Breakfasts round the big table in the dining room were always feasts, usually bacon and porridge and coffee made in the old Nelson coffee infuser. Coffee was put in jar – left side – and water in the flask, boiling the latter with a spirit lamp expelled the water into the jar and then on removing the lamp the clear coffee infusion was drawn back into the flask and, to us, didn't it just taste good.

Breakfasts round the big table in the dining-room were always feasts, with porridge, usually bacon, and coffee made in the old Nelson Coffee infuser

flat disc-shaped metal box with fine perforations to strain the coffee,—attached to pipe, with corked end for neck of flask

Coffee was put in jar—left side—and water in flask, boiling latter with spirit lamp expelled the water into the jar, & then on removing the lamp the clear coffee infusion was drawn back into the flask, and, to us, didn't it just taste good.

Father was always rather silent at Sunday breakfasts, and always used a big moustache cup, with a sort of shelf of porcelain a little below the edge, and an elliptical opening through which to drink the coffee or tea. He soon got up and retired to his study to prepare for the forenoon service. Then John would get up from his seat at the side of the table and take Father's seat at the head of the table and matters would proceed merrily or quarrelsomely as the case might be.

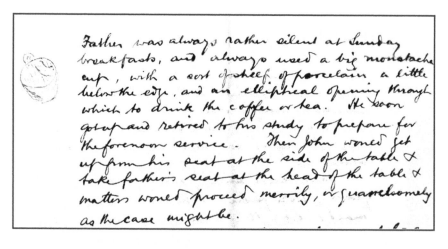

18

Then, morning service, with a good long sermon, 40 minutes or so, hearty singing in the comfortable old church. It was always well warmed. As a youngster I'm afraid I did not listen very intently to Father's discourses unless of special interest, e.g. 'on a daisy from the Manse garden' and similar titles. But I read industriously during the sermon, seated in back pew – marked in the ground plan – about the old Israelitish battles: they were so gory – tens of thousands killed on each side – in Samuel, Kings and Chronicles of the Old Testament.

In the afternoon, after a dinner – no cooking on Sunday, so it was usually a cold joint – I expect we had boiled potatoes – the afternoons were spent with reading or what we liked better, being read to by Mother, who read beautifully such things as the Pilgrims Progress, or bits from the Quiver (now defunct) or the Sunday at Home. Then we all had to memorise a hymn or part of a psalm or other piece of scripture and repeat these before tea-time.

There was either an afternoon 2 or 2.30 or evening service as well, and Sunday School, at which my good acquaintance with the Bible got me prizes every year until I too became a teacher. Baillie Chapman – a white haired man – who introduced the Orator at Bathgate last year told the company that he had been in my class in the Sunday School. I riposted that this evidently had not seriously interfered with civic advancement. Dodds was superintendent – a dark Spanish looking solicitor bearded and spectacled – spectacles always halfway down his nose.

Before him was saintly white haired and bearded Thos. Robertson – poor inspector: and another nice old chap whose fingers were twisted with joints fixed from chronic rheumatoid arthritis, who in the middle of a sentence would wipe the drop of moisture from his nose by passing his stiff curved index finger across his upper lip, assisted by an audible sniff up of air. But he was a real good chap and we liked him better than ice-cold Dodds.

The Sunday evening was the best part of the day as, to accompaniment of piano and harmonium (or organ) – one or both – we sang hymn after hymn at the tops of our voices. John giving a tenor, Father a bass, and Mother with her beautiful soprano voice leading the rest. She had a lovely voice both for speaking (and reading) and singing. She sang regularly in the choir, in the square raised platform in front of the pulpit (in plan). She sat at the near corner facing the pulpit and when I was 4 to 6 I would be with her there, furnished with a piece of paper and a long pencil to 'take notes' during the sermon. It kept me busy and quiet.

I joined in the Sunday night singing from a very early age – before I could speak properly and my favourite hymn was 'Whither, pilgrims, are you going? etc.' with the refrain, 'Trim your lamps and be ready' repeated twice, 'For the midnight chimes'. In my childish treble I rendered it thus, at the top of my voice banging on the table with my fists as an accompaniment – 'Chim shoo yamps an' be yeady … for the min yite chei'.

There was a great advantage in being one of a large family and the youngest at that. The older ones corrected the younger so that it was easier for the parents, and all the time one was absorbing things and words and phrases and ways of doing things almost unconsciously. I'm not aware of any great quarrelling or fighting. I doubt if they occurred. In fact we were almost a self-contained community content in spare time to play about the garden with our friends who were always coming about and looked on the Manse as a favourite meeting place.

Later we went about to one another's homes and altogether had quite a good time, despite the absence of organised games or school football or cricket. No tennis, golf except during our August holiday at the coast which we had every year on the Forth or down the Clyde – Rothsey, Dunoon, Ayr, Millport, Joppa, Portobello, Musselburgh and so on, e.g. Leven, Lundin Links where I first handled a golf club and on the links at Musselburgh. I first swung a golf club when I was 11 years old, so soon got into the correct swing: and once it is learned young, one never loses it altogether.

But to return. My sister Ella (Isabella Elizabeth) was only 14 months older than I was and all our lives we were special chums, getting into and out of scrapes together. Once I was wicked enough to steal two pennies and with one of these bought two red-cheeked, juicy apples which we shared. My conscience troubled me, even then, and I had to confess to Mother and the second penny had to be given up: but I had a good application of the family slipper, applied very efficiently by Mother to a tender but safe part of my anatomy.

There was a second Sunday school which met in the Church Hall, for poorer children. It was in charge of Mr Walker, father of our recent Bathgate host. He was a tall man but very nervous and shy, though one of the elect and when praying in the School, he had a funny most infectious cough between sentences, as if clearing his throat. The boys could not resist this and all over the Hall one could hear them imitating this little noise, most embarrassing but most tickling to our vivid sense of humour. I'm afraid I fell sometimes myself.

Every Christmas there was a huge tree with presents for every child: and it was a great occasion. Sometimes the presents were very attractive to small boys and once I got into a horrible scrape. There were numbers with counterfoils for each article and on the evening of the show each child drew a number from a bag, which indicated the number of presents he or she was to receive.

Well, one time there was a most attractive dulcimer, with a hammer to make music on it. I managed to slip into the hall and picked out the corresponding number from the bag before the show; and on the drawing managed to wangle it and was duly given the dulcimer. But again, my wretched conscience interfered. I got no pleasure out of my ill-gotten gains and I had to give up the dulcimer to another boy. It was a great relief to get rid of the darned thing.

...and on the evening of the show each child drew a number from a bag, which indicated the number of the present he or she was to receive. Well, one time there was a most attractive dulcimer, with a hammer to make music on it. I managed to slip into the hall, and picked out the corresponding number from the bag, before the show; and on the drawing managed to wangle it and duly was given the dulcimer. But again, my wretched conscience interfered. I got no pleasure out of my ill-gotten gains, and I had to own up, and give up the dulcimer to another boy. It was a great relief to get rid of the darned thing.

In the church when 9 or 10 I first fell in love. Next pew along from us were the Robertsons and one Sunday a most lovely dark eyed, big eyed girl appeared, a niece of the Robertsons from Melrose. I forget her name now. She was in her early twenties and married Dr Chalmers who later became Medical Officer for Health for Glasgow. I wish I could remember her name for she was one of the really lovely women I have known. Mrs Robertson was a nice old lady with beautiful white hair arranged in ringlets at the side of her head like Mother's, and she must have belonged to a fine family in Melrose, who with cousins produced some beautiful women. She, herself, when young, was a popular toast at the Melrose gathering, and in disposition, goodness and character they were just as beautiful. After all they and Mother fitted in exactly, for she was beautiful right to the end of her life.

Mother (Jane Steele Lawson) was the daughter of Christopher Lawson a jeweller in Edinburgh, who died fairly early, and thereafter she lived with an aunt, who was quite well off – a Steele. The latter married, late in life, William Finlay of a big well-known furniture manufacturer and furnisher whose shop was opposite the foot of the Mound, at 81 Princes Street, occupied later by Ballantine, Tea and Wine Merchants. For a long time I could distinguish the traces of Finlay's name under Ballantine's. They lived at No. 2 (?) St David's Street, the corner, first flat, corresponding to the first floor of Jenners. From the windows, Mother watched the building of the Scott Monument. She also remembered as a child the Burke and Hare Terror. These men used to entice poor men and women into their den in the curved street, the West Port, going down from Melbourne Place at the end of George IV Bridge, to the Grassmarket; suffocate them when drunk by placing a pitch plaster over their faces; then selling the bodies to Dr Knox, lecturer on Anatomy at Surgeon's Hall.

This was in 1828 when she was only 3 years old: so it must have been the tales about these murderers she heard later. She wore most of her life a diamond ring which her father or brother gave her aunt against an £8 loan. My brother was William Finlay named after the above. The aunt died in 1866 and with Finlay were deposited Mother's father's silver, some of it very heavy and valuable. Finlay's son, John, who succeeded to the business and made a mess of it would not give up silver in spite of my father's repeated demands for it. I expect it was not demanded with sufficient forcibleness. She (the aunt) left Mother the shop, 2 Howe Street, which at that time brought in £60 rent and the taxes were not very heavy. Now it has come down to about half. Besides the shop there are several rooms behind.

Mother was brought up very strictly: and in those days the young ladies had to spend some time daily on the back board – lying flat on the board to make their backs straight. She always had a good figure even in old age, and never wore any of the whale-boned tight corsets which were all the vogue. Yet to the end her back was as straight as a young girl's. She was rather proud of this and with a happy smile used to raise her arms covered with the usual lace shawl, and turn around to display how erect she was. The young of those days was fashionably delicate and fainted occasionally. Mother was like this. I think it may have been partly bloodlessness at times. In spite of all she was a very popular member of St James' Place United Presbyterian Church – behind the Roman Catholic

Cathedral Church in York Place. The congregation was one of the largest, wealthiest and most influential in Edinburgh and was like most UP Churches, a very friendly one, so that both she and Father, who was also a member, had numerous friends and cousins in the congregation.

She had fine features and was really good looking. Added to that she had a fine soprano voice; and was deeply and sincerely religious. To judge from the one or two letters I have of hers, sent to Father before their marriage, she did not hesitate to tick him off if she thought he needed it. She was a year younger than Father. When I was in Bathgate she could preside at a meeting and conduct the religious exercises as well, I used to think, as Father: and I used to prefer her conducting family worship, as her prayers were always so natural, easy and confident no hesitating for words or modes of expression. She lost herself in the religious exercise. It was very real to her in the end, so that she seemed to live in companionship with Christ. All her boys and girls thought there was no-one like her: though, I must say, I think she was a bit hard on the older girls, making them do their share of looking after the house and the younger members of the family. Certainly a good experience in the event of their having homes and families of their own.

She was 30 when she married in 1855 and in 14 years had 9 children – five sons and four daughters. Their names are all in the family Bible. Father was a bit of a curmudgeon about naming them ... all the girls after his own sisters whatever Mother might wish – though Willie was named after Mother's uncle by marriage and Lawson Storrow – after Mother's family name and Dr Storrow of Houghton-Ie-Spring who brought all the family from him upwards into the world.

Mother's forebears came from the Lake Country – Keswick, I think, where the name Lawson is fairly common. The great Temperance advocate, Sir Wilfred Lawson, belonged to that district and doubtless to the clan. Her grandfather Steele had a

24

shop in Princes Street about where Rentons now is; like all the others at time down a short stair, and with other things he sold toys of all kinds. There's a story of some of Father's family when very small, walking together along the street, stopping outside the shop, and the boy filling his sister's 'pinny' with toys from the stock displayed at the top of the stairs.

Jenners started as Kennington and Jenners, and Mother knew Kennington well. He gave her a very nice pebble bracelet, mounted in silver, either that or the pebble brooch which Ann now has. I'm not sure that the pebble bracelet was not received in a curious way. On the wedding morning it was discovered that Father had not bought the bride a present; and a hurried message to a jewellers brought back the pebble bracelet; quite a Shennan touch.

Father was the youngest of a family of – I think – two sons and four or five daughters. John was the elder and succeeded to his father's business of builder. He had a great idea of Mother and in one of his letters to Father said he was not sure that she was not too good for him. And he was a good brother-in-law till his death at 66 same age as his father and my father. He was Lord Dean of Guild for Edinburgh and died at a Town Council meeting.

The Finlay firm furnished everything for the new home, sending the best of everything as you could see from the remains at Downie Terrace. 'Jane was to have furnishings fit for the Queen.' The dining table could extend to 10 or 12 feet and there were two long tablecloths for it of lovely linen; one depicting the Battle of Waterloo. I remember it well.

In the dining room at Bathgate there was another solid Spanish mahogany full sized table with a heavy solid pedestal. It was dull-polished and we used to tip it upon its hinge and have games sliding down it. At the sale when we left Bathgate it sold for 16/- (16 shillings, 80 p). Fancy! One can't get such wood nowadays. It went to a joiner who would make it up into other pieces of furniture and make many times what he paid for it.

Then mother's bed was a great favourite with us boys. You remember the heavy foot of it and its shape. I first saw John put one hand at 1. and the other at 2. and vault right round between 1 and 2 from the floor, across the bottom of the bed & on to the floor again at the side of the bed. I used to do this often. And later on when I was full grown, and mother was slight & less tall, when she chivvied me downstairs I used to threaten her, and if she persisted. I would catch her up in my arms, protesting and laughing, — run upstairs with her, and dump her on the bed.

Then Mother's bed was a great favourite with us boys. You remember the heavy foot of it and its shape. I first saw John put one hand at 1 and the other at 2 and vault right round between 1 and 2 from the floor across the bottom of the bed. I used to do this often. And later on when I was full-grown and Mother was slight and less tall, when she chivvied me downstairs I used to threaten her, and if she persisted, I would catch her up in my arms – protesting and laughing – run upstairs with her and dump her on the bed.

She used to paper the rooms and I often helped her; and even in Edinburgh when over 70 she would climb step-ladders. Once at 5 Granby Road she was doing something about the canopy of her bed and the ladder slipped and she fell to the floor, bruising herself but not seriously injuring herself. I asked Prof. Chiene to see her and he gave her a good scolding.

About two or three years before she died she had gone to Alva Street and in the dark hall mistook the door down to the basement for that into the small front room – slipped through and rolled head-over-heels down the nasty stairs. This was a more serious business as she had slight concussion; and though she made a good recovery it had its effects. We thereafter never, if we could help it, let her out by herself, though she protested vigorously that she was well able to look after herself.

She had a slight lesion of one of the valves of her heart for most of her life but it did not seem to trouble her much, and at the end she had an easy and peaceful passing; unconscious for two days, and after she ceased, apparently, breathing, her heart continued to beat for several hours, so that it was difficult to know when she really passed away. I had waited on and on, but I had to go home to 95 Mayfield Road. She died a quarter of an hour after I left her on 21st March 1914, two days short of entering her 90th year. She was always uncertain whether the 23rd or 24th was her birthday and to make sure she would turn up to the last chapter of the Book of Proverbs (of Solomon) the 23 verse of which reads 'Her husband is known in the gates when he sitteth among the elders of the land' and referred this to her position as a minister's wife and so settling the day (birth) as the 23rd.

They were married on 24th April 1855 as recorded in their big Family Bible in Father's beautiful copperplate writing.

My brother, John, began his business career as apprentice to Finlays, but apparently did not take to it, though it would have been worth his while as in time he would have had control of the business, quite a famous one in its time for good solid workmanship with capable skilled employees who took a great pride in turning out good work. He went over to clerking, bringing him a larger immediate wage; but with poorer prospects. Even then, with a decent amount of backbone, he ought to have done better but I'm afraid he was not sufficiently sophisticated. That's been the failing in my brothers and myself, though I fought it better and more successfully than they did.

I remember when a kiddie of 5 or 6, Uncle Finlay promising to give me a pony if I could make a stable for it. I believed he meant it and many were my anxious attempts to see what could be made out of the big wooden clothes horse out on the green behind the church. Of course, the pony never eventuated. That was a great disappointment.

In front of the flat at St David's Street, there was a balcony over Kennington and Jenners, and either there or further along at Alex Hays similar flat at the corner of Frederick Street and Princes Street, I remember seeing the illuminations at the time of the marriage of, I think, the Duke of Edinburgh. Fireworks and every window on the old town ridge across the gardens lit up with candles. One in each pane almost. The tall 10 storey tenements on the north side of the High Street looked very fine, lit up in this way.

Much later, 1893 or so, I was in the crush in Princes Street at the illuminations for the marriage of George and Mary, when the crush was so great that many fainted and the railings near the Scott Monument were actually pushed over into the gardens. Ever since I've had a horror of big excited crowds.

(Apparent end of letter.)

You ask if there was any reaction to my first falling in love – of course not. How could there be any from a girl in the early twenties to a kid not yet in his teens? But she <u>was</u> a lovely girl, with very 'speaking' very dark, big eyes.

As I have already remarked, as a family we were very self-contained and in a way complete. To some extent this was an advantage as it was not necessary to go outside for our friends and amusements. The latter in any case were almost non-existent.

Occasionally a fair with merry-go-rounds visited the town; seldom a show like 'Pepper's Ghost' in which a ghost-like figure appeared and disappeared mysteriously on the stage. This was worked by a system of mirrors throwing the image of a sub-stage actor on to a veil of steam or smoke on the stage. It was a great thriller. Then the Choral Union had an annual concert, usually the 'Messiah' or 'Elijah'. There were no orchestral concerts, no cinema, no golf, tennis, cricket or proper organised football or other games. Father occasionally had a game of bowls – about the only 'game' allowed to ministers then. They were not supposed to interest themselves in sport of any kind.

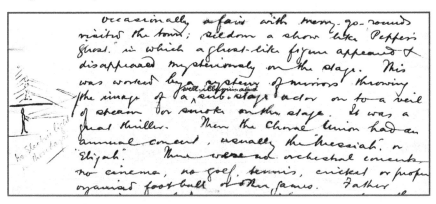

Even at school there were few and uninteresting games – rounders, leap-frog, 'bases' and so on. The lunch interval was only long enough for going home for a meal and back. Then there were home-lessons, including map-drawing on as artistic scale as we could manage. My maps were always better drawn and coloured than most others but I never could manage printing names etc. neatly and that rather brought down my standard.

But in drawing from model (casts) and from other drawings in chalk I used to do well: and at the Royal High School when in the 5th class I won the school prize for drawing, beating a boy in the 7th. But more of school life when I come to the Edinburgh School.

More about Mother. I have said something about her attractions and excellencies: but a little criticism must not be omitted. She was too much obsessed with keeping her boys and girls especially the former, home about her. That was a mistake, especially when one considers their general shyness and tendency to take a back seat. The correct thing would have been to send them out as soon as possible and force them to think and act and decide for themselves.

John, Lawson and I myself were more pushful and Lawson's and my school experiences in Edinburgh and having to go out and in by train every day mixing with others who travelled regularly to Edinburgh, and with other schoolboys in work and play, helped us a bit. But at the High School especially in the Rector's class – a large one – my shyness was pitiful. When called on to stand up and construe a portion I used to blush like a peony. I remember a boy friend beside me imploring me not to get so red; but it was constitutional and pursued me in my medical course as well, when I had to examine a patient in front of a clinic. In spite of this I did well in anything at which I had something practical to do, such as handling instruments or sponges or looking after the carbolic steam spray with which the field of operation was covered with an antiseptic cloud. I gradually got to know my way about and to hold my own with other fellows; but my hard work and earned repute as a worker helped me to hold and keep my fairly prominent position in the class and with my teachers, who were all very decent and appreciative of my efforts.

Still in many ways I was unsophisticated. 'Sophistication' is, I take it, 'knowledge of the world' and how to get on with (and in spite of possible resistance of) other people. It has something of a hardening effect on character and has really nothing to do with the things – amiabilities and good-fellowship and kindness which attract you to or repel you from other people; though it may help – by experience – in assessing these personal qualities. Sophistication is a sort of protective wall experience gradually builds up, and in the highly sophisticated it becomes so high and almost repellent and repulsive that it produces an unpleasant feeling, as if you come really not to want to know the individual personally and as a real friend. You feel there is always something held back and hidden from you.

Perhaps the best definition of 'sophisticate' is 'to deprive of simplicity, to make perverted, affected or artificial'. A sophist is a fallacious reasoner, a quibbler. So it is really not a desirable development, but what some folk require apparently as protection. 'Worldly-wise', pertaining to or experienced in the more artificial phases of life, are even better definitions, which will show you the stand to take up.

I don't mind excessively sophisticated men, but abominate the excessively sophisticated, hard girls. It has a definitely unpleasant, though perhaps not actually bad, connotation when applied to them. Display and insincerity have a part in it. They are wide awake, know the tricks and the importance of hiding the personality in the make up, so as to try to look better than nature has made them physically and mentally, and to impress others, especially the male. Another aspect it takes is the case of the masculine girl and in many of them sophistication includes also the knowledge of sexual matters, though by no means necessarily the practice of them. Although it may tend to overlay the delicacy and charm and sweetness of women's character, and it may take away much of these attributes, which one likes to associate, with women we are most fond of.

To return from this digression ...

Mother's chief and most tragic failure in this respect was with regard to my brother Alexander. His father intended him for the ministry and with that in view he took after 3 years' study – the Master of Arts degree (MA) of Edinburgh University. But he was so shy that he couldn't look at the idea of the ministry, and perhaps it was as well, though this was the profession most suited to him, and even on the moderate salary he could have married and brought up a small family to be independent. So he went in for teaching and had some experience of this in Edinburgh schools, but again shied at the difficulty of keeping order and disciplining a class either of boys or girls.

Then he joined a coaching business, for postal tuition, and did quite well in this for a few years, till the boss either died or failed and the business stopped. It was carried on in a former shop in Abbeyhill just beyond Regent and Royal Terraces and looking on to the end of Calton Hill, at the east end of these Terraces where they join. Meantime he was doing some private coaching as well, and at that time the usual payment was 1/- *(one shilling, 5p)* an hour, so we had to do a lot for our money.

Then, as Lawson was doing pretty well at dentistry, someone – I forget who – suggested that he might qualify in dentistry so as to assist Lawson. He got through the Edinburgh course at the dental hospital and after having his Diploma we thought he was fledged: and proposed, and argued very strongly in favour of going away from home to be assistant to some dentist in a good practice. This would probably have made him, strengthened his character, made him independent, and put him in the way of earning a decent livelihood. But Mother simply would not agree. 'You wish to take my son away from me.' So, willy-nilly, he remained at home, not getting far away from feminine influence and associations, and with natural softness unaffected and uneradicated: helping Lawson, doing work very slowly, and without self-confidence, niggling at preparing a cavity, and making dentures in the workroom carefully and well, but as if he had a whole lifetime for each case. Too much interested in the unessential things of life and failing to develop character and independent thought.

Lawson was offered an assistant surgeon's post at the Dental Hospital which would have kept him in the front row of dentists in Edinburgh and attracted patients but, you will hardly believe it, he refused on the ground that it would involve giving away the knowledge and experience he had picked up in Philadelphia at the University of Pennsylvania, where he got his DDS. He did not appreciate the advantages of constant rubbing up with the other surgeons and with students with their constant questions which he would have had to answer by reference to literature and others' experience. These were the all important wrong moves made by these two, which as you now appreciate altered their whole lives and made them approximately failures, instead of successes.

Of the girls, Jessie, who died in 1884, and Ella who died in 1905 (1906?), had most personality. Jessie born in the year Queen Alexandra came here from Denmark to marry the Prince of Wales and in consequence having the additional names Christina (after a sister of Father's) and Alexandra after the Princess, so her full name was Jessie (another aunt) Christina Alexandra. Lex has her silver spoon – presented after birth by these aunts with JCAS engraved on the handle. Irreverently and in fun we dubbed her JaCkAsS and she retaliated promptly and suitably.

Isabella Elizabeth (after the other aunts – Margaret was named after Aunt Margaret) also had a presentation spoon – dessert size – with her name engraved, also in Lex's possession, along with some more of Father's silver which I rescued from the Downie sale especially a very heavy soup ladle and an old fashioned fish slice, both with hallmarks dating them in the early twenties of last century (1800s).

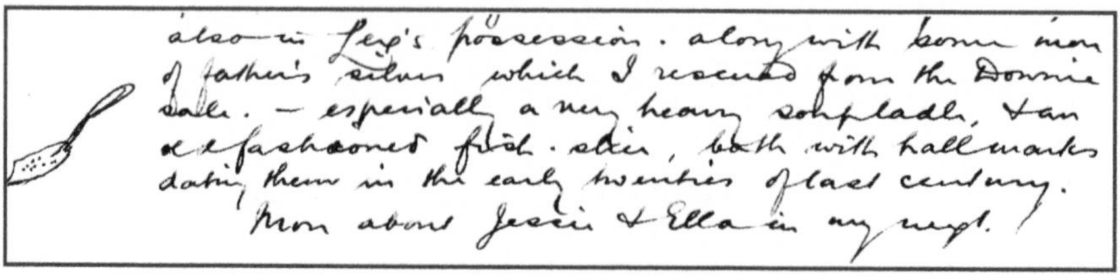

More about Jessie and Ella in my next…

(End of letter.)

25 Fonthill Ter
Aberdeen
Mar 31. 1940.

My dear David,

The pages I send you this time
cover some of the saddest and hardest
experiences of my life and it is
something of a relief to get them done:
the failures, misunderstandings, the
wrong directions taken are I suppose
common to every life; but it's a
pity we can't see further ahead &
avoid the mistakes. For example
children even now have a better
chance of survival and the gross
danger of tuberculous milk has been
cleared away, to a great extent, though
not completely eliminated.

I am glad you saw Edward.
Have you given him these memoirs
to read, or does he want to do so, &
will he be sure to return them if
sent?

Well, little Jean's 4th birthday
comes on April 5th. How time flies
& how she is lengthening out. She
bathes & dries herself now & can
dress herself in a way. At least
she thinks so, but yesterday she

35

31st March 1940

(The pages I send you this time cover some of the saddest and hardest experiences of my life and it is something of a relief to get them done: the failures, misunderstandings, the wrong directions taken are I suppose common to every life, but it's a pity we can't see further ahead and avoid mistakes. For example, children even now have a better chance of survival and the gross danger of tuberculosis milk has been cleared away, to a great extent, though not completely eliminated.)

Jessie easily had the best brains of the family. She was brilliant; had imagination and poetry in her being so different from the rest of us. She was keen on languages, French and Italian chiefly, and on poetry, and very good at music. She was a favourite pupil of Carl Hamilton, then the chief teacher of pianoforte in Edinburgh, and he thought so highly of her that he got her to play with him at a public chamber concert in Edinburgh. At times she seemed almost fey, and able to see and know things hidden from the rest of us. Once she told me she thought she saw angels' wings in the sky. She was distinctly spiritual. She drew well too, and painted beautifully on china, beautiful delicate flowers, forget-me-nots, delicate grasses and tendrils which seemed quite naturally to fall into place in the design.

Her death in 1884 when 21 was a calamity, as, had she lived, she was bound to have made a big name for herself and to have become a leading women of her time. She had the ability, the personality and the force which would inevitably have taken her to the front. Her portrait, by Robert Gibb RSA which I now have and which John had made from a small photograph, shows well her open eager fine face (*this portrait is at Grove Lodge*).

The fool of a doctor in Bathgate sent her off for a holiday to Houghton-Ie-Spring (Durham) with her left chest full of fluid. Mother was not satisfied and took her to see her own Edinburgh doctor, Dr Alex Sinclair, who put her at once to bed in the

Shennan's house in 24 Fettes Row (?), and drew off 80 to 100 ounces of fluid which had compressed the lung and pushed over the heart, so that it had difficulty in functioning. When she came home weak and an invalid, she was able to come downstairs. She tried to play her beloved piano, but her fingers would not take the lovely runs, and in despair, she said to Mother 'Oh Mother, my fingers have lost their cunning.'

It was a sad day for me in May (20th) that I came home from the High School in Edinburgh to find that she had passed gently away. That was the hardest break I had in our family, except perhaps the parting from Ella, who was my special chum. Ella was more like Jessie than Jean, very lively and frolicsome: always seeing the bright side of things and trying to make folk happy. She had not such good brains as Jessie but did well and worked hard. We had many grand ploys together and never wearied of each other's company. She was a real brick of a girl. James Kesson – Lawson's great friend – was very fond of her and her death was a heavy blow to him. Perhaps that is why he never married.

With several of her great friends – Jean Watson and Bessie MacKintosh (still living in Edinburgh?) and one or two others – she went for 6 months or a year (1890 or 1891) to study music and pianoforte in Leipzig. There she had 'flu or a bad cold of some sort, from which she never properly recovered and was probably badly treated. I used to write her regularly from my assistantships in Broxburn, Lugan and Gorebridge, and once wrote that I was a good deal bothered with Effie Lenzie (2 Influenza epidemics). She did not see the joke and wrote to Jean, very much worried as to who this girl was Effie Lenzie – who was bothering Theo.

Mother took her about 1899 or 1900 to the States to stay with John at Great Falls, Montana, to see if the climate would improve things, and she stayed there for about 6 years, always, I fear, longing to get home. I went across for Mother in 1901, and met her (mother) and John at Chicago, about halfway between Great Falls and New

York. I had a stormy voyage to New York but on the way home with Mother the sea all the way was like a millpond. The captain, a jovial Clydesider, set her at his right hand and every meal used to tell her very tall stories in an attempt to shock her: but, in vain, she gave as good as she got; and I think they were very sorry to part. She was 76 or 77 then.

The captain wore a very heavy gold ring, a presentation one, heavier and wider than mine, with two big diamonds on either side of an equally big yellow one. Some of his smoke-room yarns were enough to raise the roof. I remember one or two of the more shocking.

Ella, after gradually getting worse in spite of the change, came home in April 1906, travelling alone the 2500 miles to New York, and then even farther to Glasgow. I don't know how she did it, or arrived alive. I went through to Glasgow to meet her. I fancy it was in the old NBR Queen Street Station Hotel, and I did not recognise her, she was so changed and haggard and only when she came to me and called me by one of her pet names for me did I realise who it was. I was dumbfounded, but did the best I could (it was a Saturday night with holiday crowds) got the guard to lock us in a 3rd class compartment by ourselves, but it was a worrying time till I deposited her at 5 Granby Road, Edinburgh, behind our house in Mayfield Road (95) where Mother was living at the time.

She lived only a week after getting home, and was full of hopes to the end. I was holding her in my arms when suddenly she cried out, 'Oh, Toddie, I am dying,' and she was away. It just about broke me up. We had always been so much to each other, and had been parted for 6 years; and her just to come home to die. Both (Ella and Jessie) died from the damnable – though preventable – disease, tuberculosis.

Well, that's rather a sad section; but the next year 1907 was worse still – also in May, the 12th – when wee bright Ivy died from the same disease but in this case contracted from drinking un-sterilised milk from tuberculous cows. A thing I had been writing about very strongly from 1899 onwards. In spite of our care, a careless housemaid gave her raw milk. Only two glands in her abdomen infected, but the disease spread from there to the spinal cord and up to the brain. She lay unconscious for 4 weeks, and you cannot possibly realise what that meant to her mother and myself. It changed the whole of our lives and inevitably made me harder and more rebellious against the 'slings and arrows of outrageous fortune'; it gave such a feeling of insecurity in all things as if nothing were worthwhile anymore. *(Photos of Ivy, including of when she was ill, have gone to the archive at the University of Aberdeen.)*

We left home, sent away our maids, and went into lodgings in Buccleuch Place and also at West end of the Meadows for a year. It was a mistake, because coming home again just freshened up the ache and sadness. Dr John Thomson, the leading children's physician in Edinburgh and in Britain, and Dr Graham Brown, Physician to the Infirmary, did their best, but from the first, as treatment was then, it was hopeless.

Dr WG Sym, the leading oculist, a good friend, who had lost a child in similar circumstances, did not comfort me much by telling me that life would never be the same for me, as if I did not know that already. She always ran to her daddy out of harm's way, or from teasing, and the last things she played with were her favourite 'Daddy's pennies' sovereigns from my gold sovereign container at the end of my watch chain. They are still somewhere about, in my desk, wrapped up and marked 'Ivy's pennies'. There is a sketch of her I made while she was lying unconscious, in the long drawer in my desk; and also a song her mother used to sing to her 'My Treasure'. It began:

Only a baby small
Dropped from the skies
Only a laughing face
Two sunny eyes

and ends

> Only a baby small
> Never at rest:
> Small, but how dear to us
> God knoweth best

You can understand how we couldn't bear to look at it again, remembering how wee Ivy liked it. She was the picture of sturdy babyhood, strong, bright-coloured, with slightly darkish hair, not brown, with bright shiny golden ends. It looks too dark in her photo. She was only 2 and a half years old, but was very advanced for her age. She walked when only 10 months old and could talk quite well when 2 years old.

She liked a joke. Once at table, on her mummy's lap, she looked round at us. 'Granny, got white hair, Mummy got brown hair,' then across at me, 'and Daddy, none hair' raised a great laugh at my expense. Dear Wee soul. I haven't forgotten her for a single day since then.

And what a tragedy that you weren't allowed to have an older sister, who would have made everything so different, and so much more pleasant for you. May has been a bad month for us. Father died on, I think, the 24th, 1891. (*Hay Shennan says 13th May, and see later.*)

There was a curious incident after Jessie's death. One of her great friends – a Miss Brook, I think – was very ill at the same time, and probably of the same disease. A day or two after Jessie's death, this girl became unconscious, apparently moribund for quite a time. On regaining consciousness she told her folks that she had been in Heaven, and had asked why such a talented girl as Jessie Shennan had been taken, and she was told the reason. At the time she said it was quite satisfactory, and the answer had made her quite happy; but that on coming back to earth, or to consciousness, she could not recall what the reason was. She, too, died shortly afterwards. But the communication, regard it as you like whether credible or otherwise gave Mother and Father great comfort at the time. I relate it for what it is worth. It may go to show that we should not or need not grieve too much over the passing of our beloved ones, believing that death is not the end of all, and that there is a happy, useful state, free from all worry and trouble on the other side, where vital activities are continued in fuller measure than is possible here below.

The black baby grand at Downie was bought for Ella by Mother for £60 – through Carl Hamilton. It was a superb instrument when new.

Jessie taught me my earliest music, and the notes on the piano; and I had no other lessons until with Lawson I commenced violin lessons with Jas Winram in the late nineties. But I gradually increased my facility by strenuously playing away at simple hymn and psalm tunes and gradually progressing to those in keys with more sharps and flats. Jessie played and practised on Mother's old upright cottage piano which had a wooden frame, across which were stretched the wires a couple, if I remember correctly, for each note, in place of the present 3 on the iron framed modem pianos. It was by Allison, London. The more difficult and complicated the piece, the better she liked it.

That piano stood in the dining room to the window side of the door, and it has another memory for me. I remember well lying on the carpet on my stomach, with my head underneath the keyboard, trying to settle what I was to be – an artist or a doctor. Finally, actually I tossed up a penny, and it came down every time for 'doctor'.

In a similar position I used to pass hours reading an old leather-bound folio volume of Xenophon's Anabasis, in the original Greek with all the queer old contractions and symbols which were then like an open book to me. I was 15 or 16 and wish I could do it now. Greek literature is super excellent and when I began to dip into Plato, I was enthralled.

At the old Manse, there were always folk coming and going and the highlights were on anniversaries and soirees connected with the church; when sometimes 4 to 6 brother ministers would meet together, and make the evenings merry with song and story – especially the latter.

But I must get on with things.

Mother as a rule took things – even sorrows – very calmly, so great was her transparent trust and confidence in an All Wise Providence overseeing, controlling and guiding all things. But there comes a time to every woman, at the end of the child-bearing period, about 50 years of age, when great internal upsets and dissensions occur in the body, depending on the throwing-out-of-gear of the important internal secretions. These upsets are in some cases serious, and upset and blind the judgement leading to queer, sometimes hysterical outbursts. Mother did not escape and poor Father had a rotten time for a year or two. When in these turns she would accuse him of all sorts of things, and ill-doings: and he got very exasperated at times and responded very sharply and severely. So that it was not at all a happy time for those at home.

Even after she recovered, things were a bit spoilt between them, and when in 1885 a woman came to her with a highly coloured tale of how Father had behaved to her daughter, she believed her against all Father might say. I was in the house at the time and heard Mother wail that he had disgraced his family, etc. etc. I believe it was something quite simple and innocent in trying to comfort the girl who was in trouble, but the old harridans, of both sexes, lay and clerical, believed it all, took it to the Synod and Father was deposed. By this time it had so preyed on his mind that he became melancholic and in a way mentally deranged and was unable to put up a fight of any kind.

John, however, to his everlasting credit, was old enough, 29 or 30, to realise where it would land us all and took legal advice in

Edinburgh: and the legal folk ferreted out the real facts and made their mightinesses in the Synod eat their words and publicly recall their judgement. What awful hypocrites some of these beastly saintly ministerial friends (?) of Father's were, especially a fat-paunched flabby chap, Reverend Barlas of Musselburgh, who had protested with tears in his eyes that he would stand by Father through thick and thin. The d......d humbug.

A damnable experience for us all: but thank the Lord we struggled through it to the light once more. And there's this to the credit of the Bathgate congregation. They all with few insignificant exceptions believed in Father, Mother and in us all and we kept their kindly affection to the end. I think in their eyes Mother always wore a halo and Father's memory was kept green. One consequence was last year's request to me to be Orator, and Ann and I were received by high and low like a Queen and King: old wifies breaking ranks from the crowds to shake my hand, and old chaps coming to swap reminiscences. It did me good.

I believe, however, that Mother to the end retained something of a hard feeling towards Father's memory and we buried him with his own folk in the north-east corner of St Cuthbert's Churchyard in the Shennan burial place and not in the one at Bathgate. In addition, even though we were then in Edinburgh, 1891, and I was earning an income and so were the other boys, we did not feel brave enough to face a Bathgate crowd.

The last pages give accounts of some of the worst times I've had to fight through. You and Edward have so far been saved from such harrowing experiences: but they come sometime or other to all, in varying degree, and you have to steel yourself to overcome them and not be too downcast, knowing that to the faithful doer, a fall is always followed by a rise again to ... if not to full happiness.

Reading back over what I have written about Jessie, I find I have forgotten the folk she was to stay with at Houghton – the Carrs.

43

There were three girls Alice (Jessie's special friend), Ella and Beatrice. Alice was about Jessie's age, Ella about Lex's and Beatrice was two years older than me.

Ella was the beauty, with lovely dark expressive eyes in a most attractive face. She was very dainty, of medium height with small and fine hands and feet. They were always very nicely dressed and all the accessories were just right. I remember Ella used to wear shoes of what are called I think the monk's type, with a wide heart shaped tongue in front which accentuated the smallness of her high arched feet. I was devoted to her and once brought her shoes to her, while they were with us down at Clynder on the Gareloch. I dropped them quick, for a wasp which was in one of them fastened on my finger and stung me. But I did not much mind as that had saved her from a nasty experience. She had a very small waist, after the fashion of those days, and one of the finest figures I have seen. I doubt if Lex has retained their photographs.

After Jessie's death, John got engaged to Alice because she was his favourite sister Jessie's friend, but they were never really in love with one another. Jessie was the bond and after a time it was broken off. That was one of John's mistakes. He should have gone for Ella who was very fond of him and would have stuck to him for life, and what a lovely, attractive wife she would have made.

There was another Houghton family, the Lishmans, and Alice nursed one of the boys and generally looked after him for years. He came to Edinburgh later for the medical course. Broke down in health some years after graduating and went to live and practise in Madeira, and actually married Alice who was so much older than he was. I haven't heard of any of them for many years – 40 at least.

Beatrice was our Ella's friend and the object of my first sustained love affair. She was not so pretty as Ella, as she had a somewhat roman rose which spoiled her otherwise nice face and profile, but for the rest she had the beautiful figure, hands and feet of her sisters. She was very fond in a way of me, and we kept up correspondence for years; but she was cold, never let her affection blossom out, and gradually became high churchy and one of the chaste nunlike character, devoting herself to church work – they were Anglicans – and went to Peterborough where she became a nurse or deaconess giving up her life to good works, and practically became a member of a sisterhood abjuring all sex and such matters. The last I heard of her was that she was a district sister at Seaham Harbour in County Durham and I do not know her later history. So that was that, and a bit of a disappointment to me. They were of the very best.

Ella married some chap in business in the East, and her honeymoon began on board a steamer with her newly married husband. She would have changed the whole of John's life for the better had he had the sense and knowledge to choose her.

It just shows how small are the influences which determine our destinies.

John had many other nice and physically attractive girl friends, e.g. the Forrests of Glasgow, relations I think also of the Bathgate Robertsons. Fine upstanding, well educated and, for the time, sophisticated women, and again always well dressed. But he seemed to miss his mark somehow. Perhaps he had too many girl friends, and too few men ditto, though he was quite a man's man for all that. More so, for example, than Lex. Lawson was, first and last, a man's man, finding most of his friendships among those of his own sex. I'm afraid I was responsible for putting him off his one love affair, with Jessie Longbottom. She as a soft lump. I did not like her name, but she had plenty of money. They were fond of each other and might have married and all to Lawson's advantage. I regretted it ever after. He would have had an easier life, and an easier ending, poor chap. It shows how dangerous it is to come between people. A couple should always be left to settle their own lives. It was, as it turned out, one of the worst things I have done.

I think cousin James W Shennan had a great idea of Jean at one time but it did not come off; and at one time there was almost an understanding between Lex and Bessie MacAlister – daughter of a Free Church minister at Auchterarder – but Lex was never in a position to make an offer to any girl.

You must not think too hardly of Mother after what I have said, for at these times, the best women are not responsible – at least fully – for their words and actions and there's no doubt that taken all together she was one of the best mothers possible and performed marvels on a very small income, a thing impossible or almost impossible now-a-days.

I sometimes think of that journey to Chicago, wakened by the dark attendant of the sleeper, the breakfast while speeding along the shores of Lake Superior – the waters stretching away to the distant horizon. And glistening in the sun, the huge banana, the mush (porridge), the rolls and lovely coffee; the toddy at Chicago, Niagara and the passage beneath the falls, the bridge to Goat Island, and standing over and looking down on the huge horse-shoe Canadian falls, the suspension bridge, the oyster stews in the restaurant in 23rd Street, New York. When I returned in 1908, New York had quite changed, and I couldn't find my way around so easily, but I visited Battery Point and its aquarium with those extraordinarily bright-tinted fishes and so on.

As you have gathered, Father was really non compos mentis during the last six years of his life, and he seemed to shrink into quite small bulk. He was for some time at Dumfries Mental Home. Sometimes at home where he was very helpless, wolfed his food and dribbled his drinks, and latterly at Mavisbank near Dalkeith where he died, with the mental shadows and depression deepening: the saddest end for a man of good intellect and brain-power that can be.

It was a relief to us all when it was over. I don't know how the expense was met: it may have been from the Aged and Infirm

Ministers' Fund, as Mother had nothing to spare, and I was going through the Medical Curriculum, which must have cost a bit, part of which was met by John and part from my earnings as tutors to schoolboys. You can fairly well understand why I am and have always been very careful of money, doing without things I should have liked, and saving all I could. In comparison you two boys have had and will have easy-going all your lives. Apart from a gift of 100 Preference Shares in Green's, I've earned every penny I've spent all my life.

From the time 1886 that we went to Edinburgh, Mother kept the house going by taking in boarders. She had nothing else till Father died when she got about £400 from his Life Insurance, except about £30 or so from the Howe Street shop; and we managed somehow all right. Till 1889 – three years – when John went to America, he gave her some help but all of us earned a little by coaching or by the girls holding classes for youngsters. We were first at 12 Sylvan Place overlooking the Merchant Maiden's Hospital on the grounds of which later the Sick Children's Hospital was built.

On going to a top flat – new then – 76 Thirlestane Road almost opposite the Baths in that road, we sublet Sylvan Place and got into trouble by the sub-tenants turning out to be loose immoral women who had men in and messed up the beds.

Once when alone in Sylvan Place, a buxom girl from the dairy nearby came in with some milk and hung about for a long time, evidently wanting me to pet her or more, but I was too innocent at the time to appreciate her wants and I did not rise to the fly.

We were in Thirlestane Road for about three years before going to 71 Leamington Terrace (which led up to Bruntsfield Links, and the tram line to Morningside along Bruntsfield Place), a huge house with big rooms and large basement and a rent of about £75 a year. We stayed there until 1900 when we shifted right across to Newington near the station to 35 Mayfield Gardens where, as at

Leamington Terrace, I carried on a practice at the same time doing research at the Royal College of Physicians Laboratory, assisting Cathcart at the Museum of the Royal College of Surgeons, and Bruce, the Lecturer on Pathology at Surgeons' Hall.

I soon became pathologist to Leith Hospital and to the Sick Children's Hospital and in 1899 took over the Lectureship from Dr Bruce. My income from all these things came to about £600 a year, and I went in for 95 Mayfield Road, buying the house in 1902. When I married in 1903, Mother and the others moved to 5 Granby Road and after about 5 years to 6 Ventnor Terrace off Mayfield Gardens, looking on to the Suburban Railway near Newington Station.

All these years in spite of difficulties we paid our way and even had many pleasant times, golfing on the Braids, skating on Dunsappie or Dunningston, etc. etc.

(End of letter.)

Father was born August 1st 1824 and died May 13th 1891. His mother was Margaret Lamb who, in later life, suffered from night-blindness, so that she could hardly see her way about. Her parents were William Lamb, Builder and Wright, of Tyningham, Haddingtonshire (1734–1809) and Margaret Thomson, his wife (1737–1818) who (the latter) introduced the night-blindness (retinitis pigmentosa) into the connection. They had a family of 10, 4 sons and 6 daughters. Margaret lamb was the 9th of the family. The sixth of the family, a son, also became blind in later life.

Dr C Usher found out for the paper we wrote jointly on the Incidence of night-blindness in over 300 of Margaret Thomson's descendants to the 7th generation, that 'she was regarded in later life as being mentally affected when in serving the porridge she poured it not only into the actual bickers but also into any receptacles on the table such as tea-cups and bread plates. Surely her action might be ascribed to defective sight.' Her sixth child (1772–1850) a builder in Leith 'was always referred to as "blind Peter"'. (Hay Shennan in his record of the family says his name was Patrick.) He was a great friend of my grandfather – John Shennan – and Hay thought that it was almost certainly in his house that John met his future wife – Peter's sister.

Three of Peter's (Patrick's?) sons and two of his grandsons developed the same night-blindness.

Two of Father's sisters, the oldest member of the family, Margaret (1809–1888) and the second youngest Isabella (1822–1900) became almost completely blind latterly. Aunt Isabella Hume (Birkenhead) had five children, 4 male and 1 female. One male, the eldest, was deaf, and the three youngest, 2 sons and one daughter, became blind. The second youngest is Alexander Shennan Hume (named after my father who baptised him), 5 Euston Grove, Birkenhead. He was an actuary in Liverpool till he had to retire on account of the sight defect. He married a very nice-looking and pleasant Irish lady – Annie Robinson – and had four children. The oldest, a girl, died in infancy; the two surviving daughters Norah and Kathleen are very good looking but have never married. Martin, the son, is married and has a small family.

Aunt Isabella's eldest son, James Hume (the deaf one) married Margaret Knox who became blind. They were first cousins, Margaret being daughter of one of my aunts (Christina) who showed no blindness, but she died fairly young in British Guiana (Georgetown). (Hay says she did suffer from night-blindness.)

James and Maggie Hume had 4 children, two of whom (males) became night-blind, and two girls, one of whom died at 7 and the other, Isabel, now the only survivor, is deaf. The older son was Edgar Hume (James Edgar H.), husband of the Minnie Hume you know, the younger, Kenneth (William Walter Kenneth H.), joined up during the last war and was killed by a sniper at dusk, not being able at that time of day to see his way about.

The night-blindness usually appears about 50 years of age, sometimes before that, again in the case of Kenneth Hume; and the deafness is quite often an associated condition in others of the family in which there are night-blind members. It runs in families, transmitted sometimes by mother, sometimes by the father.

A curious thing came out in Usher's and my investigations. One of Father's uncles – himself unaffected – and whose descendants, 139 in number, in 5 generations, most of the 3rd to 5th generations now living in New Zealand – did not hand on the trouble and none of the 139 was or is night-blind: but one only of his sons was deaf. He, the latter, had two sons and two daughters deaf out of a family of 9; but none of the great grandchildren or great great grandchildren has ever been deaf – so far as we could learn, up to 10 years ago (1930), apparently the tendency having become suppressed possibly by infusion of new blood by marriage. Night-blindness is an hereditary defect and probably different from the variety due to lack of vitamin A, which is curable by administration of that vitamin.

You really should go to see the Humes at Birkenhead.

The condition can be transmitted sometimes by the mother, sometimes by the father. Father, his children and grandchildren have escaped.

Father had two brothers and five sisters, that is a family of 8. His father was a builder and wright in Edinburgh, at first as Shennan and Walker, later on his own, and his son John succeeded to the business. They lived at first at 24 Gayfield Square, off Leith Walk, and later in Haddington Place. Then they moved to Bellevue Cottage in London Street.

Gayfield Square is back to back with Broughton Place UP Church where a famous Dr John Brown was minister. He was Father of Dr Brown of 'Rab and his Friends', and of Professor Crum Brown whose class in Chemistry I attended. The minister's father was the still more famous Dr Brown of Haddington, a copy of whose huge annotated Bible, with illustrations, I kept out of Father's library. It is in the bookcase in the dining room on the window side. Father's pulpit Bible, and family Bible, with family records are above the other bookcase.

Lex confirms that the Shennans lived at 24 Fettes Row, First Flat, and Aunt Margaret with the Knoxes at 22 Annandale Street. Jessie was taken to Fettes Row, to the Shennans, and not to Aunt Margaret's, who by that time was blind.

Later on when and if I reach the tale of my medical course, I'll tell you more about Professor Crum Brown and the extraordinary set of Professors I was privileged to study under.

Dr Brown of 'Rab and his Friends' lived I think at 19 (or 21), Rutland Street, opposite Caledonian Station. Later it was occupied by Dr Alex Peddie, another UP and son of the Manse. I was christened by Dr William Peddie, either a brother or father of this Doctor – probably brother – as he was pretty old when I consulted him about Father, during the latter's later years.

Father's mother – Margaret Lamb – died in 1857 when the family (remains of it) lived at Bellevue Cottage. John Shennan occupied the lower flat and his mother and sisters occupied the upper flat. Father was married in 1855. The cottage was below the level of London Road, on the site now occupied by the Catholic Apostolic Church, and John's letters to Father and Mother before and after their marriage are addressed from the cottage.

His family, (Jim, Hay, etc.) often spoke of their happy times at the Cottage, and this is elaborated in Hay's record, a copy of which I made, and which you can read at any time. John and his father did a lot of building in Edinburgh and in the country, and Father told me that they had some hand in the building of Brodick Castle on Arran. (Hay mentions other property that they built.) Perhaps my skill with tools descends from my grandfather and the generations before him, at Tyningham and at Auchencairn in Galloway.

Aunt Margaret was a dear wee soul – all her brothers and sisters were tall and well built: and Hay relates how once she was very angry with her brother John and said 'John, I could kick you.' John at once fetched a chair, lifted her on to it, and turned his back. The ill-humour very rapidly dissolved in laughter. Without exception they were a happy, good humoured crew: and Jim and Hay fully inherited this happy disposition.

She (Aunt M.) was full of kindness and happiness. We always liked visiting her and never came away without something in our pocket. On one occasion Lex and Lawson were leaving, and she gave each what she thought was 1/- *(one shilling)*; but Lex got only 1/2 *(6d)*, whereas Lawson got 1/-. He often chuckled over that, because, of course, Lex could not well tell her she had made a mistake. Her great grief was leaving Edinburgh for Birkenhead to stay with one of her married sisters there. She used to sing very sweetly a song about Love for Edinburgh which always brought the tears to her eyes. She died 1888, 79 years old.

Her nephew, Willie (Arthur) Knox, who lived with her in Edinburgh was a rolling stone, and a bit of a rotter, who never was much good: though very pleasant in person and manners. He was trained as a carpenter, and his birthday was March 8th. The Knoxes' mother (Christina Graham Shennan) had gone, when she married William Knox, a great friend of John Shennan – a glazier, when in Edinburgh – to Georgetown, British Guiana, where her husband had a good business, so far as I know. Hay says that Christina suffered from night-blindness. They both died, comparatively young and the children, Margaret, Jeannie and Willie, were brought home to be looked after by Aunt Margaret. Father was one of the Trustees in the estate for years, and all his business letters connected with it are carefully copied in two letter books which are somewhere about the house. It was not an easy or pleasant Trusteeship. Total value of this Trust was nearly £37000. The children were difficult and quarrelsome. The British Guiana 'entires' which I have – in a long drawer of my desk – came from this lengthy correspondence – chiefly 1862, 1863 and 1864.

Maggie Knox used to come to Bathgate to look after the house when Mother was away, and we did not like her much because she was too strict and stingy.

She became Mrs James Hume – Liverpool and Waterloo – and died 8 years ago or thereabouts. Jeannie, always deaf, was kind and decent, and a constant correspondent of my sister Jean to the end. Of that whole generation only Alex S Hume, Birkenhead, survives and is well on in the nineties, but still plays his beloved violin.

John Shennan, my uncle, was Lord Dean of Guild of Edinburgh and, like his father, died of heart trouble suddenly at a meeting of the Town Council. He was a real good soul, father of James (father of Oswald Shennan) and Hay, the Sheriff (father of Alison and young Jim) and Maggie Gibb, wife of Robert Gibb, RSA His Majesty's Limner for Scotland, who painted the famous 'Thin Red Line' now owned by Dewars Ltd, the whisky firm, who own also 'The MacNab' by ?? Raeburn, another famous painting more than life size.

R Gibb was a great favourite of ours – for golf and for good stories. We often visited him at 2 Bruntsfield Crescent, looking north on to Bruntsfield Links – just across from Leamington Terrace. They were a fine couple, but unfortunately childless. He had a magnificent mezzotint of the painting of Law – 'Lord Newton' – grand massive head and shoulders in his judge's robes. His studio was at the top of the house, but he let no-one in to it, except models. Hay Shennan e.g. sat for one of the figures in the 'Thin Red Line'. To get proper impression of the shot horse which is falling in the foreground, he had one shot to see how it would fall. The picture was an inspiration. Once when out walking near Fairmilehead, he suddenly seemed to see the whole picture, as if in action, in a field on one side of the road. Maggie became blind almost completely in later life.

Father's generation, and the older members of their families were quite a crowd in Edinburgh, cousins and half-cousins, and all in good circumstances: Shennans, Knoxes (Humes, later Birkenhead), Lambs, Hays (Alex. Hay, Jeweller in Princes Street), Nisbets (SSC, 24 York Place). Teenie (Christina) Nisbet was a great friend of Jean's and of the Lowes, another fine St James Place UP family – plumbers and electrical engineers. Teenie and Miss Low took Jean for a holiday to the Harz mountains and she greatly enjoyed it. Ella lived with Teenie when she was at school in Edinburgh at the same time as I was at the Royal High School. Mr Nisbet (pere) was co-trustee with my father in the Knox estate.

Then among their great friends were the Drummonds. I often heard of 'Bertie' Drummond, son of Dr Drummond, DD, who succeeded Dr Logan Aikman as minister of St James Place. The last named married father and mother. This Bertie Drummond became minister of Lothian Road UP Church and is now the venerable Dr Drummond, you know. His wife, a very fine woman, was well off. Your mother knew them well and she and her brother Joe used to visit them often when their house was on the East side of Archibald Place off Lauriston. Your mother lodged in Forrest Road, and Joe in Lauriston Place.

They had a daughter, Joan, and a son, who is a missionary in India. Joan, from a leggy rather ugly child, grew up into a fine-looking graceful woman, became head of the girls' Guildry of the Church of Scotland, and could conduct a large meeting as well as her reverend seniors. She married Rev. Mr Thomson, an assistant of her father. He became minister of East and Belmont Street, Aberdeen, and he and his wife were quickly much thought of. They had two nice boys. She died quite young. I was responsible for settling the diagnosis of cancer, to the universal sorrow. Thomson soon returned to Edinburgh to North Mayfield Church. He died a few months ago.

Your mother used to tell a tale of Joan and her brother. The two were out walking and Joan heard a very foolish lady remark, 'What an ugly child.' She asked her brother, 'Am I really so ugly as all that?' 'Well,' he responded, 'you're not so ugly as Satan, you know, Joan.' All that was really wrong was her complexion, which was muddy, spotty and sallow. She had good features and dashed good grey matter.

The name Shennan is undoubtedly Celtic in origin, and our forebears were among the Scots who came across from Ulster to Galloway – others went to Argyll. The ancient race were the 'Seanains or Mac-Giolla-t-Seanains of Ireland'. The Kintyre (Argyll) branch was known as MacOsennage or McOshenag, as appears in documents of 1505 and 1547. The Galloway form was Aschenan under various spellings. A is the Gaelic Ua and the Irish O, meaning 'descendant of' and the first 'Scottish record of this name is in 1309. They had lands in Wigton and Kirkcubright; near Loch Ken and near the present village of Lauriston. Others were at Gatehouse, but latterly the concentration was at Auchencairn near Dundrennan, and Rerwick. In the churchyard of the latter there is a group of tomb-stones to the memory of our forebears, usually 'Shennan' but also spelt 'Shennon' and even 'Shannon', the Irish form of the name. Those in Auchencairn or near it were either farmers or wrights, and one was a Clydesdale horse breeder (Shennan of Balig). There was a Shennan of Park for many years (16th Century) probably near Shennanton, on the main road about 5 miles west of Newton Stewart. My grandfather was a wright and came to Edinburgh from Auchencairn and Hay and his brother and sisters kept up the friendship with cousins and half-cousins who remained there, and an Aunt Shennan.

There is a prosperous family of Shennans in New Zealand. One was at Cambridge University about 1916.

Above is taken from Hay Shennan's Record which is too lengthy to quote in full. It gives very interesting details of our forebears, going back, actually to 1066, 'The Irish records mention MacSeanain, Lord of Gaileanga, who was killed in that war and four of his successors down to AD 1145.' This would probably be the origin or the Irish variant Gilson. I think the Irish 'Sean' is pronounced 'Shen'.

Hay could not trace our pedigree further back than my great-grandfather whose defaced tombstone was replaced by Hay's father in 1866:

'In memory of John Shennan, Farmer, who died at Auchencairn 1817, aged 77 years, also Janet Donaldson, his wife, who died at Barlocco in 1809 aged 70 years. Also Margaret their daughter who died at Standingstane in 1795, aged 25 years.'

Ann and I visited Auchencairn, Dundrennan and old Rewick Churchyard in 1935. Quite near on the Solway Firth, is Maryport whence Mary, Queen of Scots left for England after her defeat at Langside. In 1935 there was a Miss Shennan still living at Dundrennan and the same year when signing our names at Burn's Cottage, Alloway, we noticed that a Mary Shennan living somewhere near Stranraer had visited the cottage only two days previously.

Up to comparatively recent times, most large families in Scotland – at least the parents – had the ambition that at least one of the sons should grow up 'tae wag his heed in a poopit'; otherwise should enter the ministry, and that is probably the feeling that, in part, influenced Father to go in for the study of Theology. He, himself, wanted your Uncle Lex to follow his example.

In those days it was not deemed essential to take the Master of Arts (MA) Curriculum at the University, and he entered the Theological College of the UP Church which had some quite notable Professors. He was well acquainted with Latin, Greek and Hebrew; and during our school days he was a great help to us in our studies of Latin and Greek. He could consult all in the original texts.

Before that stage, however, he had some business training, and acted as Teacher of Writing and other subjects in some of the schools in Edinburgh, especially young ladies' schools. So that he started with a fairly wide culture and had many friends. In St James Place he had a men's class, or Bible Class which thought much of him and when he married gave him a collection of 50 books, most of them fully bound in calf. I have about a dozen of them still – Histories of Scotland etc. I think the large collection of the green-blue cloth-bound book of Bohn's Library were almost amongst the 50 books. I have the remains of these.

He was well respected in the congregation, as was also Mother, and the marriage was regarded as a natural selection by both. They were both deeply religious and were in sympathy in all things connected with Church life.

Perhaps, in a way, Father as the youngest of the family had more consideration than the rest and, of course, there was mutual love and adoration between him and his sisters. I suspect, however, that his big brother John tended to keep him in his place and was not backward in making his opinions evident, though all the same he saw great possibilities.

I have no records of his life before he married, except a tale I often heard of him as a youngster and which Hay also retails:

John Shennan, his father, had a strong sense of humour, which made his home a happy one: and he was by no means a 'heavy' father. When my father was very small, his father had punished him for some fault or another and the child resented it, perhaps thinking he had been treated unjustly. At bedtime the small boy said goodnight to each of the members of the family present, except his father, whom he ignored. Then just as he was going out of the room either his conscience pricked him, or his sense of filial duty inspired him, and he turned and said 'Goodnight, Father, I fancy.'

We often used this phrase, as youngsters in saying goodnight to Father and he rather enjoyed the joke.

Their 12 1/2 years in Houghton-le-Spring were happy ones, even though the salary of a dissenting minister in England was then small. They had many gifts in kind from relatives and from friends in the congregation; made many life-long friends; and when he left for Bathgate, he was given a big gold watch with suitable inscription engraved inside. Lex wore this until he took over Lawson's gold Hunter after the latter's death, and sold Father's watch for the value of the gold.

He took the Bathgate charge, partly for the better educational facilities for his family, and partly to be nearer his native Edinburgh and the surviving members of his family. This was in 1867, and almost immediately he came up against trouble – a bad, damp, manse; a stubborn, unfeeling and intransigent Kirk session; and political animosities. He had even to vote as his session decreed.

In 1870, he was favourite candidate for the London Road UP Church in Edinburgh, but unfortunately he had to preach his trial sermon just after Maggie's death and while Willie was seriously ill (he died in April of the same year, Maggie in January).

He was so worried that in his sermon he lost the thread of his discourse and broke down. Ministers in those days had to preach without notes. So he failed, and this had the effect of breaking his spirit and lessening his ambitions. Such a little is required to influence a career.

John and Willie both went to the Royal High School, where Jim Shennan also was: and John often had to stand up for Willie, who never was strong. Once in the class of mathematics under Munn, who also taught me, Willie had been unjustly punished, and John vehemently objected. Then followed a lively chase of John by Munn over the benches: but I did not learn the ultimate result. His uncle, John, was the same: he was the fighter in his school.

I have been looking through Father's old docketed papers and found a request from the Factor to Edinburgh University for payment of arrears to the General Council in 1867: so that Father must have been a University man and likely a graduate as only graduates are members of the General Council. But to my recollection he never signed himself MA but he was a member of the General Council.

He had a call to Whitby at the same time as to Bathgate.

I also found receipts for payments £4 a year to the No. of England Dissenting Ministers' Widows Fund, and that I now remember brought Mother £26 a year from 1891 when Father died to 1914 when she died; so that was a help added to the £30 or so from 2 Howe Street shop.

It is more than likely that Father also went to the High School. John and Willie were there about 1868–70 at the same time as Sir George Adam Smith and Hay Shennan was Dux in 1874. His close rival was Professor WP Paterson who had the Divinity Chair here (succeeded by Curtis, now in Edinburgh and Fulton). He went to Edinburgh and was Dean of the Faculty till a couple of years ago when he died, full of years and honours. I knew him quite well and he used to remark on Hay's often just getting in front of him.

The UP, the Free and most of the branches of the Church of Scotland in England united long before the Unions in Scotland to form the Presbyterian Church of England. Some of the principal Church of Scotland branches and off-shoots, e.g. St Columba's, remained as congregations of the Church of Scotland in England.

(End of letter.)

18th April 1940

Lex has been up to the University and consulted the Librarian and the search informed the latter of something he had not known viz. that by the University (Scotland) Act of 1858 students who had attended four sessions were allowed to qualify for the Membership of the General Council. Father took Law in 1842, and Literae Humaniores (Latin and Greek) 1845–8. He was a member of the General Council. He was a member of the General Council 1864–5, 65–66 and 66–67, but did not compound the fees and so did not become a life member. He paid up 12/6 in 1867 and another 7/6 would have done the needful: but in those days every penny had to be carefully watched. Still by doing without 2 or 3 books he could have done it.

In one calendar the name was spelled 'Shenann'.

Now, before going on, some information from letters to me in the nineties from Mother, Ella and Jean:

From these, it seems clear that my sister Ella was in good health until she went to Leipzig in 1891. She had some sort of respiratory inflammation there, which was apparently not treated sufficiently. At all events she was never the same thereafter, and came home with an ache in her side and shoulder, almost continuous. It worried her greatly all her life and she had lost weight. The letters tell of visits to various places, especially to Blair Atholl and Forres where I went to pick out comfortable lodgings for them. I think that for a time she was with Mother at Forres Hydro.

Then she went to John at Great Falls, Montana in 1899 or 1900 and I went for Mother in April 1901. For two or three years she progressively got worse. How she managed the home journey I cannot tell. It must have been purgatory. There was a rumour in Great Falls that she had died at sea, and John had to correct that in the newspapers. She came home one Sunday and died the next Saturday, 6th May. That day and on Sunday the 7th, John in

Montana felt restless and uneasy, full of foreboding, knowing that something serious must have occurred. He took up the hymn book which lay on the piano just as Ella had left it. Every Sunday the two used to sing for an hour or two, at least John did, to Ella's accompaniment. And my cable did not give him the shock it might have done as he was prepared for it.

I came across John's letter to Mother on the sudden death of his wee son from Diphtheria in 1893. He had had to leave Alice and Tot in San Pedro to come to Great Falls, on being kicked out of the Arizona Copper Company; and they had been left in the best of health and spirits. He and the kiddie were great chums and played together a lot; and he had this terrible wire when thousands of miles away. You can imagine how broken heartedly he wrote. I couldn't keep the letter; it was too tragic, reminding me too much of my own experience, and I destroyed it. These are the blows that change one's whole life.

In other letters there is a lot about our difficulties, of the risk of taking the large house at Leamington Terrace, of the offers by friends and acquaintances of boarders, etc. One from Lawson, saying he was going to have no more shilly-shallying about Lex, wasting his time tutoring and he had made up his mind to make him go in for the Dental Course, as he himself was then doing well: and that was the start of A Shennan LDS.

There was also docketed in Father's handwriting an Essay on the Ten Plagues of Egypt by Lex, when a student in MA classes 1882–1883. Quite good and quite in the sermonising style! Showing that he could have written good doctrinal sermons and, of course, showing that he should have been made to go in for the Church. So easy to be wise after the event! (Lex tells me that he has forgotten all about this.)

Now a letter of John's to show what a different person he was before he went to America. During all the nearly 50 years he lived in the Western hemisphere he had misfortune, and he was too honest and simple-minded and kept up his religious instincts instilled during his childhood all his life. But he was not sharp enough and sufficiently alive to his own interests to fight the sharpers and unscrupulous men he met in business; and they did him down in spite of the repeated financial help I gave him.

The letter was written while I was a student, and we were living at Thirlestane Road. Evidently the others had gone to Pirnmill on the West side of Arran for the month, and he and I were alone at home. I had made my breakfast and gone off by an early train. He writes from the Arizona Copper Company's office which was then at 74 George Street.

3rd May 1888

Dear Theo, After you bolted this morning I had my breakfast. What way did ye no mak a sup parridge? Man, I got awfu' tim (toom, empty) aboot 12 o'clock. I've been baad ever since and I'm no to get to Lamlash (Le. on East side of Arran) the nicht and somethings I ordered hevney come and I'm like tae sweer and the Karnarey (anglicised 'Dickie') is at the Johnston's and it's come on rain and Jock's (the dog) at the Hamiltons and I hope to go down the morn at 6.20 but preserve us a' it's awful sin (soon) and I'll have tae take my breakfast the nicht and I'd better no gang tae bed at a' and the best laid plans o' mice an' men gang aft agley and Amen and that a'.

The postman body brocht a scribble frae Mither and she wants me to bring down Jean's gown a yelly ane but I'm no sure whether its recht or wrang but there's one away by the post this forenoon only I've just sent half of it, the ither, the better half namely the body couldna' be fand – it was absalom – absent I mean.

Mother says their travelling expenses were £1:18:6 – surely this is wrong, it is nearly Bleach, and if correct how did you manage with only 9/6 or so – like Pat did you take it out in 'walkin'? The wardrobe and all the doors are locked and the keys put under the bell on the lobby table also the front door only it (the key) is not under the bell but here. I won't come up again till Wednesday and will probably return to Lamlash on Thursday for a day or two longer and will see if can't get round to your side of the island.

Love to all, Jack.

That's a jolly letter, full of the joy of life. What a change after the nineties began.

Ella had an awfully nice friend Maggie Stanger staying with us at Pirnmill. She was an Orcadian, short, fairly plump but nicely made, bonny and I have a pencil sketch of her in one of my sketch books. She was a trump and enjoyed our larks together; but at that time and for years thereafter no thought of special affection for anyone of the other sex (except, I remember, Beatrice Carr) entered my head and though she was evidently fond of me and Lawson it never even occurred to us to return her fondness, or even kiss her. She married fairly young and died young to Ella's great grief, quite possibly, as so many Orcadians go, from Tuberculosis.

One of my great pleasures was going out for the night into Kilbrannan Sound with the herring fishers; then they were bathing and boating and climbing the hill behind Beinn Vhann – I think it was. As I have already told you we had the Carr sisters there too, as well as at Clynder on the Gareloch.

I remember seeing John off to America at the old Caly Station on the 3rd September 1889. We were great friends for many years and he did a lot for me to help me through my medical course. Without that help I could not have managed it. I was earning only enough by tutoring to keep myself clothed and to pay occasional fees. I had no bursary and there was no Carnegie Trust in those days.

Thinking back on those happy times makes me wonder if I have been too hard with him during the past 10 or 12 years, and made too much of saving for my family.

But one month, I sent him £75 and £40 – and that was only a portion of what I sent. Still I don't want to excuse myself. I think the first ten years here were the most anxious, knowing that if I died there would be no provision from the Varsity for my own family, or for Mother and those in Edinburgh. I had to help: Moreover, if I had gone ill and had to retire during these ten years I should have had no pension.

Nowadays things are better, and for the present professors the insurance not only provides a pension but some provision for widow and children. Even now my pension ends with me, and the Varsity under the arrangement I came under has no responsibility thereafter for my widow and children. Only the Scottish Ministers and Professors' Fund to which I have paid since coming to Aberdeen and which will bring in something like £55 or £57 a year to my widow. You can understand something of the urge to save, that made us – your mother and me – do without things and many years without holidays, and with very little travel. When you're married you've got to consider these things.

Professor Carroll is responsible for detecting the dangers of the old Varsity pension scheme and for working out actuarily the new and better and fairer scheme which takes into consideration the dependants.

Leamington Terrace was really taken (1889) to serve as a good professional spot for Lawson to start. That was before he went to Alva Street. He came home from the States at end of 1890 or beginning of 1891. It was a pity as he could easily have made a big income in the States: and lived well and prosperously and been able to help the home folk more than he ever was able to do, as it turned out. But Mother, and we all, were wanting him to return, which was perhaps a mistake: even though Mother always maintained that she would never stand in our way, whatever we decided to do or wherever we were.

Leamington Terrace was also to serve for me for Mother was sure that I would make a success of practice in Edinburgh and I was getting on famously before my inclinations turned to research, teaching and museum work. My income from practice was doubling or nearly so every year. I think I had not sufficient confidence in myself and was afraid that some horrible mistake might dish me as a practitioner. I expect every Doctor has the same fear: but with me it was a persisting obsession, or remnant of the inferiority complex which so plagued me as a youngster.

I think this may lead me to say more about my own life and progress; referring in the course of it to the other members of the family, or to friends, teachers or colleagues as they impinge on the narrative.

One thing impressed me from an early age and it was a mistaken idea. It seemed to me that whenever I made a close friend or chum of a boy I seemed fated to lose him by death: and ever after it made me shrink from getting to friendly or intimate with any lad of my own age.

The first was a youngster of 6-8 – Willie Russell – son of a shopkeeper near Aitkens in Hopetown Street, and he died, a great shock to me. The last was Willie Hutton, son of the parish minister of Oldhamstocks, Haddingtonshire, quite near the Berwickshire border. He was my great friend while I was a student and I passed long holidays in their manse, an always welcome guest, for I had a great fund of fun and anecdote in those days, and most enjoyable they were – with tennis at the surrounding farms – all gentleman farmers, dancing and all the rest. I was almost engaged to Nellie his youngest sister. He died in 1899 and the obsession haunted me almost all my life and interfered with possible friendships.

I doubt very much if, as a youngster at school at Bathgate, I had

66

much inferiority complex. I fancy it was the other way around. I felt all the time that mentally I was better than most of the other boys in the class. It was in most instances a mixed class: the head boy and head girl standing together and other boys and girls each keeping to their own side of the crescent facing the headmaster. In the senior classes the sexes were taught separately in some subjects. I specially remember Jessie (?) Alexander at the head of the girls in the French class, standing beside me. On one occasion there was a great guffaw when she confidently translated 'Merci, Merci' by 'Mercy, Mercy'. Even then she was a trifle deaf. Lex visits her and her sisters in Edinburgh. She is now very deaf. I haven't seen her to my knowledge since I left Bathgate Academy.

My great rival was James Hunter, son of a dairyman at bottom of the Parish school entry and he shared the first prizes with me in our last years – I think six each, but he got one that I was sure I should have got, as I was confident I was better at the subject. I fancy it was Greek.

He could draw a marvellous horse with a stroke or two of his pencil and wrote very neatly. He had a constant discharge from one ear, and was very short tempered – I realise now that he can't have been very robust. Lawson and Jim Kessen once teased him so that he turned on them with his fists. He was not a great fighter, and the two rascals were so tickled at the idea of James Hunter fighting that they laughed themselves helpless, and could not resist him. I believe he is a teacher somewhere in Scotland.

I was always on top in Sunday School and that made me feel uppish too. I found memorising and other homework easy. Perhaps it made the drop all the greater when I came up against my equals and superiors intellectually at the High School. Still there were some things even there, that I could do as well as or better than others: and I enjoyed my three years there though I was not allowed to play football or to do rifle shooting, but I played cricket and was quite expert in the gymnasium – with

Sergeant-Major Parker. In my last year in the 7th class, a swimming bath was built in one of the front annexes; but I never learned to swim. There was no proper instructor.

As a matter of fact I left the Bathgate Academy, somewhat of a prig: and I had a lot of that knocked out of me at the Royal High School. In Maths I had Munn, the same who chased John over the benches 13 or 14 years earlier. With a sweep of his arm, keeping the shoulder steady, he could draw an almost perfect circle on the blackboard. He had two sons in my class, the older of whom, not at all smart, became a doctor and ran for years a mental home near Norwich. I'm almost certain he was Lord Mayor either before or after your grandfather.

Dubourg, our French master, was a great favourite and did us well. Von Ravensberg, the German master, was by repute a <u>Count</u> in lowered circumstances. He used to jabber away to us in German, but only a few of the smarter boys picked up much from him. I won a prize in my class, but I'm afraid it was not altogether deserved, and I never had a good grounding in the language. On his desk he always had a tumbler into which he put some drops of a yellow fluid before filling up with water. He sipped this during the lesson, but we never made out what it was.

Old Cranstoun taught Classics, especially Greek. He was another great favourite though we used to play pranks on him, e.g. piling up the fire so as almost to roast him. At that time he was putting together a classical Atlas which I believe was a monument of learning. He lived – almost alone – in Bright Crescent, off Newington Road and Minto Street, and for years after I left school I used to look in on him and I kept some of his letters tome for a long time.

Practically all the masters wore black stuff robes and mortar boards.

The English master, a slight, athletic chap with a keen ascetic face, a perfect gentleman, had us in the hollow of his hands from the start. His learning was so apparent that he at once impressed us, as also did his neat way of dressing and 'clean' look. He was the one I referred to in 'The Orator Looks Back', as reading to us the Ancient Mariner. I have written the present Rector to find out his name and if I get a reply promptly I'll put it in (Mackay, John).

Thomson Whyte – who was second English master when I went to the RHS and became senior when the man I mentioned went to Liverpool – was a huge man well over 6 feet, strongly built and always wore a frock coat with fairly light grey trousers. He had a twinkle in his eye, and was really gentle, belying his appearance of great strength. He of course as was usual then, wore a short beard. He was a good teacher but not so brainy and intellectual as the other.

He had a boarding house for the boys in Portobello like several of the others. To see him running across between classrooms, with his gown and coat tails flying in the wind, was a treat.

Dr Marshall, the rector in my time was a very highly cultivated chap with a keenness for the Arts. He painted in oils a bit. He knew his work well – chiefly Classics – and took the senior classes. He gave an impression of snobbery to some extent: not being the 'natural' gentleman like the English Master: but he was very decent to me.

Lord President of the Court of Session Inglis presided at the prize-givings, and gave us our prizes. He was a most impressive looking old gent, sitting in his robes under the white marble bust of King Edward VII who attended the school when a boy: at least received tuition from the Rector (Dr Schmitz). John Edgar was another classics master whose favourite studies were Horace and Ovid. Unseen translations were his forte and we had plenty of them. He wore big spectacles and rather puzzled us for a time by checking mischievous boys by name even although at the time he was writing on the board with his back to us. By and by, we found out how he did it – the reflection in his glasses against the black surface of the board.

There were no severe punishments at the Royal High School though old Cranston had his cane (I think) but hated using it and others had the strap or tawse. I doubt if I got a single 'palmie' at that school though I had had plenty at Bathgate.

We played cricket in a fine field between Holyrood Palace and the Holyrood Brewery with a road and stretch of pass between the south side of the field and Arthur's Seat. The Prince of Wales (Edward VII) had obtained it for the school out of Royal property, in memory of his attendance at the school. Sir James Purves Stewart, of whom you have doubtless heard – a physician, Westminster Hospital – was a pupil at the same time as me, though not in my class and was heartily disliked. He was always eating sweets and chocolates and we dubbed him 'sugar doodle' a nickname that stuck to him when a student of medicine. He wrote his reminiscences lately. I once travelled with him from London. He had been at some evening function and had on all his decorations, orders and medals etc. Keeping open his Inverness cape he promenaded with me up and down the platform just to give people a treat. That was when I travelled in a First Class sleeper.

There were two brothers Umpherston, Frank and Charlie. The older was an ugly little chap but he could clear the horizontal bar at a height greater than his own measurement. The younger one, better looking, a mischievous tease and good runner went into Law and was Sheriff or Sheriff Substitute in Fife, if I'm not mistaken. Latta, a quiet studious tall, pale-faced boy in my class became Professor of Logic in Glasgow University and was the Glasgow Secretary of the Glasgow – Aberdeen Senates' Golfing Society for years after I began to play in the yearly meetings. Harrower was his opposite in Aberdeen.

For three years, 1883–6, I travelled daily the 18 3/4 miles between Bathgate and Edinburgh (8.05 a.m. and 3.40 or 4.20 p.m.) getting to know Edinburgh well, so that when we moved from Bathgate in October 1886, we were at once at home: and straightaway I began my medical course.

Lex was at the Varsity, Lawson at Daniel Stewart's College, and I was at the RHS during the 1883–6 years. We had a lot of fun on these journeys. A chap, Sinclair, a clerk, went out and in at weekends, and brought back his jam pots for refilling. He was, of course, dubbed 'Jeely-cans' – many others not worth referring to.

Only once did I miss that morning train in three years. One other morning I had bacon with plenty of hot fat to my breakfast and developed the most appalling migraine all day. I could see only half my field of vision and was practically useless at work. Another dark morning I had dressed in a hurry and only when I was nearing Edinburgh, discovered that I had on long stockings of different colours – I wore short knickers, with button or elastic below the knee in those days. The fellows were very decent. They must have noticed the blatant stockings but I was never twitted about my mistake.

The Edgar I mentioned became a Professor at St Andrews at a later date in the nineties. An old friend of mine met him a week after his appointment and asked him if he was making many friends in the town. He answered, 'Oh, the professors keep strictly to our own circle,' or something like that.

Another teacher's face – JK Duff – was always covered with pimples and little pustules. He was a decent chap but was nonetheless dubbed 'Plukes' or 'Plukey' or 'Pewks', variants of the Scots word for pimple: he could however lay on the tawse hard.

Some of the 'old boys' used to come about frequently and get to know youngsters in the playground. There was one – I believe one of the Sandersons of Leith who used to bring a miniature bagpipes and play to us. Looking back I fear that he must have been 'saft a bittie'.

We were taught to revere the memory of the old boys like Sir Walter Scott, and Lord President Inglis, the latter of whom I have mentioned as presiding at prize-givings. Sir Henry Littlejohn, Hay Shennan. But the number of famous old RHS boys is legion. Jas Nasmyth, Lord Jeffrey, Lord Cockburn, etc. etc. Sir G Adam Smith, Boswell, Drummond of Hawthornden; the Adams – famous architects; Stevenson – engineer; Lord Brougham, Archbishop Tait and McLagan and latter's nephew Sir Douglas McLagan – Professor of Hygiene at my time; Syme, the great surgeon, father-in-law of Lister; the three Monroes, father son and grandson who held the Edinburgh Chair of Anatomy between them for 120 or 130 years. Erskine, Lord Chancellor of England, etc. etc. (and, of course, Professor Shennan of Aberdeen!!!).

My last prize in the 7th class was Boswell's Life of Johnson in three volumes 'for general excellence'.

I think it must have been while I was at the RHS for we were still in the old manse, that I managed to make enough, by drawing and painting Christmas cards and other things, to buy my first pair of long trousers, 16/- or 16/6 (16 shillings, and 6 pence) made to order. I was a d..... d fool. They were made all right but I thought they were too baggy in the legs and in a secret session somewhere upstairs probably in the loft – I proceed to narrow them and made a thundering bad job of it. They must have looked queer but I wore them out all right after sundry re-alterations.

Father used to buy our suits at Hyams in the High Street next to the Tron Church; and an ordinary charge for a boy's suit was £1 or £1.1/-. Of course everything, or most things, were cheaper in those days or we couldn't have got along at all. In a way it was fortunate that we moved to Edinburgh in 1886 for it just fitted in with my being ready to start at the Varsity.

My RHS days were pleasant ones, as John was in digs in Cumberland Street, and later on Lex dossed with him; so that was one constant port of call; another was the office of Waddells Contractors, who built the first Mersey Tunnel. There I became acquainted with the mysteries of the telephone and early attempts at electric lighting and was made the butt of jokes over the phone by John's colleagues in that office. That was 35 St Andrew Square (east side of square! They are now in No.21 or were in 1909), now next door to, and north of, the recessed head office of the Royal Bank of Scotland, and close to the original warehouse of Coffee Laws – now in Princes Street.

Then there were the cousins in Annandale Street and Fettes Row, and later Jim Shennan's house after marriage – in Nelson Street; before he became well off and went to the Hermitage near Granton Harbour. Teenie Nesbit in 21 York Place at west corner of the street going up to Clyde Street and the garage where we put up when staying at the RB Hotel. John and Miss Low in 27, Mayfield Gardens (for two years we were in 35, Mayfield Gardens, 1900–1902) and the cheeriest, nicest folk you could imagine. Miss Low such a gentle sweet little soul – the very best. And there were others and we were welcome at all these houses while the 'clan' and St James Place Church were still going strong. Almost all the connection has died out. There remain only young Jim – son of Hay – and Alison his sister, and Oswald, son of Jim Shennan. John

Rognvald, Hay's elder son, is in south west Wales. Of our own crowd, of course, only Lex remains in Edinburgh.

Ella was with Teenie Nesbit, and I acted as courier and porter between her and Bathgate.

We played golf as frequently as we could on the Braids Hill course, opened about 1884–5. There was either no charge or only a small one, 3d *(3 pence)* or so: and in the winters we skated on the pond at Blackford Hill or on the lochs in the (then) Queens Park. This continued till the close of the century. Thereafter a long cycle of mild winters started, so that I haven't had on my skates for 40 years; and I was quite a performer – doing a lot of figure skating.

I passed my preliminary General Knowledge exam when 15 years old, very easily: and next year for the fun of it sat it again – English, Latin, Greek, French and Maths. For going in twice I was hauled up before Professor JR Fraser Dean of the Medical Faculty, and had some difficulty in explaining just why I had done it. However, I got off lightly with a very light reprimand.

Logic was an essential for the MD and I forgot all about it till about 10 years later within three weeks of the preliminary exam before the date of handing in my MD Thesis in 1895. I had to go to little Tero, a queer little communistic chap, but very brainy. He managed to put as much logic into me as stuck until the exam was over and passed. That was a narrow squeak. Dynamics and physical geography were other subjects in the first prelim. I passed. But classics and French and English literature and History were dead easy to me in those days. I wish I knew now half as much Latin and Greek as I knew then.

I began in Summer with a Botany class at the Botanic Gardens at 8 o'clock every morning, and I had to walk from Thirlestane Road near the Grange Road. Only horse trams in those days and not much good when one was in a hurry. Old Alex Dickson whose portrait is in the big Tercentenary volume of the Edinburgh University 'Quasi Cursores' with my other professors was the professor of Botany and he received us after lecture to take our fees, with a huge cigar between his teeth. The professors took all the fees and paid their assistants and stood all the expenses of running the departments. They must have made a good thing of it at 3 or 4 guineas each – no, I believe it was 2 or 3 guineas each then – in classes of 250 to 400.

Patrick Geddes – the noted town planner, who lived in and extended the Ramsey Gardens on the Castle Hill, and ran the lectures at the Outlook Tower just outside the castle gates, was his senior assistant. He had a big nose and a regular mop of hair. I have a sketch of the top of his head somewhere, as he leant down over the lecture bench, something like that in the margin. You saw just the conical nose emerging from the mop, parted in the middle line. He was a great friend and collaborator with Arthur Thomson the Aberdeen Professor of Zoology, and I frequently saw him here and met him occasionally.

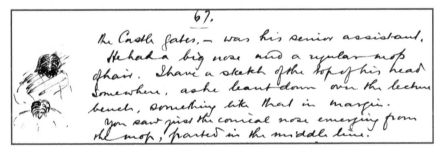

The name of the of the English master at the RHS was Mackay (John H.) and he left when invited to become professor of history in Univ. of College Liverpool – now University of Liverpool.

The Professor of Zoology was Cossar Ewart, prof. in Aberdeen before Nicholson who preceded Arthur Thomson. He was a tall rather handsome man with piercing eyes and black hair. He was unlucky with his wives; two died young, or at confinement, and he was about to marry his third. He had a breeding farm for horses at Penicuik where he experimented with cross-breeding, with zebras I think.

When here he built that red granite house in Rubislaw Den South opposite the top of Anderson Drive. At that time there were no houses between it and Queens Cross. He went to Edinburgh in 1882 or 83 and died only 2 or 3 years ago – must be more 8 or 10 *(written 1940)*.

He was not a popular teacher. He was or seemed very unsympathetic and cold-blooded. I think he was English. The thing that stands out in my memory of dissected frogs, and crayfish and earth-worms and skates was his remark while we were dissecting a cow's eye. He described its structure and ended by saying that in his opinion the eye might have been designed much better. It sounded to us almost like blasphemy.

We had no Natural Philosophy which proved a distinct disadvantage, even although I had learned a little of it in Dynamics. It was a pity for we would have been taught by that great physicist, Tait, who shared the top of the Physics tree with Lord Kelvin (Glasgow). He was the father of Freddie Tait, the great golfer – gutty ball – who was killed in the Boer War. He worked out graphically and mathematically the flight of a golf ball and the distance it could carry. Freddie when next playing disproved the whole thesis by driving a ball farther than the limits his father and worked out. Freddie's sister was the wife of CW Cathcart, my first chief at the Infirmary and College of Surgeons.

Crum Brown – brother of Dr John Brown, author of 'Rab and his Friends', son of Dr Brown of Broughton Place U.P. Church (whose father and grandfather were famous divines located in Haddington) – an old High School boy, was Professor of Chemistry and had the most profound intellect in the Senatus of great men. He had a deep knowledge of maths, physics, philology, a marvellous knowledge of ancient and modem languages – including Russian and Chinese, in which (latter) and in Engineering he set Exam papers.

He it was who worked out relation of graphic formulae to chemical structure and composition and worked at problems of varying atomicity. With JR Fraser (Sir JRF of the chair of Materia Medica) he investigated connection between chemical constitution and physiological action of salts of ammonium (alkaloid) bases; and his investigations of the sense of rotation and its relation to the structure of the semi-circular canals of the internal ear were famous.

It was claimed that he could, if necessary, lecture, without special preparation, on any subject of the curriculum. Old Sir David Macalister, principal of Glasgow University, came nearest perhaps to him in the wideness and universality of his learning; at learned gatherings of scientists from all over the world (D. Mac.) was said to be able to address most of the delegates in their own languages.

'Crummy' as we called Crum Brown would have been over 6 feet if he had not had such a round back that his big head seemed sunk on a short neck between his shoulders. He had scant hair but a full beard and always wore a black velvet skull cap. He had a thin squeaky high pitched rather slurring voice, and gesticulated while he spoke quickly, looking up at us with his bright lively eyes. The huge classroom reached two storeys up in banks of seats and it was always full. He always began the winter session by putting high up on a shelf in the right corner above the platform a 1000cc beaker or measuring glass to show a diffusion experiment. A blue solution being carefully run in below superjacent water so that at first a sharp meniscus separated the liquids: and during the term we watched the gradual mixing of the layers.

69.

'Crummy', as we called Crum Brown would have been over 6 feet if he had not had such a round back that his big head seemed sunk on a short neck between his shoulders. He had scant hair but full beard and always wore a black velvet skull-cap. He had a thin squeaky high pitched rather stirring voice, and gesticulated while he spoke quickly, looking up at us with his bright lively eyes. The huge class room reached two storeys up in banks of seats and it was always full. He always began the session by putting high up on a shelf in the corner above the platform a 1000 cc beaker or

As a class of first years always does, we treated the wonderful genius badly: and over and over again he would threaten that if we did not behave he would cut out his most interesting experiments, e.g. burning an iron rod in oxygen, which was received with great enthusiasm, and so on. Of course we stupids did not appreciate till later what a great man we had to teach us: but how proud we became later of his achievements.

He was very keen on sulphur experiments and Doctor, later Professor, James Ritchie (Bacteriology) wrote a text book with R Muir, the popular 'Muir and Ritchie'. They composed a most witty skit on the activities of all our Professors. He pictured Crummy coming to the nether world and being questioned as to the work he would choose to take up. Ritchie, imitating Crummy's squeaky voice in a stammer, made him suggest that 'he thought a very good research would be "on the allomorphic modifications of sulphur"' which of course brought down the house; as the materials required would be to hand, in the nether world.

I wish I could remember a tithe of the tales that were current in my time about the really great men in the Senatus of that time. They don't make such men nowadays.

I did not work well my first year, and came a cropper in my first professional in, I think, Chemistry: the only exam I ever failed in.

That one experience made me pull up my socks and for the next three years I worked hard. The course was then four years, and as it turned out I did not lose any time by my failure. The non-medical subjects did not intrigue or interest me greatly.

I was keen on Botany at the start but boggled at the great detail demanded: the same being the case with chemistry which was chiefly Inorganic. We got very little of the organic and nothing of the physical.

In fact, compared with what present day students get in their 1st year in Biology, Chemistry and Physics, our instruction was distinctly elementary: and I suffered from this all my professional arid teaching and research life.

One of the RHS games was Bases, played in the schoolyard. Two lines were marked out about 20 yards apart: one side stood between and their job was to catch the others as they raced from one base to the other. Little Umpherston was one of the most difficult to catch and another was a rather unpleasant chap Rose, belonging to a Baptist family your mother used to visit when a student, in that street below Calton Hill and Royal Terrace – along which the trams from Leith Walk run to Abbeyhill – north of the hill.

I am not sure but that this Rose or a brother was the Sir Arthur Rose, Chairman of the University Grants Committee of the Treasury who died recently. On the gravel of the playground this game was tough on boots and clothes.

About 5 minutes time by a footpath down the hill below Regent Road to Holyrood took us to the field.

When I was at RHS there was a stairway down to the Waverley Station at the corner between GPO and the old North Bridge. This disappeared when the bridge was rebuilt – mostly of steel curved arches, built girder-like, between the piers.

(End of letter.)

8th May 1940

As I proceed you will appreciate the high calibre of the professors and other teachers of my time: many of them of worldwide reputation quite as high as that of their predecessors in the end of the 18th century and first half of the 19th – the three Monros and Goodsir in Anatomy; Sir Robert Christison in Medical Jurisprudence and Police (i.e. Forensic Medicine and Public Health); Laycock and Cullen in Medicine, also the Gregorys; Hughes Bennett in Medicine and physiology; Sir Charles Bell, James Syme, Liston, Lister and Spence in Surgery; Sir James Y. Simpson in Midwifery (he introduced chloroform). Bennett was a rabid opponent of Lister's antiseptic treatment of wounds which has saved many millions of lives.

My lot, in addition to those I've already mentioned on former pages, were Sir William Turner- Anatomy and later Principal of the University; William Rutherford in Physiology; Sir J.R. Fraser, Materia Medica; Sir Douglas Maclagan and Sir Henry Littlejohn in Forensic Medicine and Public Health; Sir Thomas Grainger Stewart in Medicine (Physician to Queen Victoria); W. J. Greenfield in Pathology; John Chiene, Thomas Annandale, John Duncan, Francis Caird (later Professor), Charles W. Cathcart, J. W. Cotterill and lesser lights Miller, Maclaren and Macgillivray in Surgery. Sir Patrick Heron Watson and Joseph Bell were a bit passé, but both had been brilliant surgeons and physicians, with Crimean War experience; and both were good friends of mine.

Extra-murally there were Sir John Halliday Croom in Midwifery (son of a UP Minister, Lauriston Place Church), along with Berry Hart, Brewis, Freeland Barbour, Milne Murray and Frank Haultain – all also in Midwifery and all prominent among their fellows. M Murray invented the well known and much used axis-traction forceps for assisting delivery in delayed or obstructed cases.

Diseases of the eyes were in the hands of Sir Douglas Argyll Robertson; Mental diseases in Clouston's hands; etc. And there were others well and widely known like Sir Byron Bramwell, John Wylie, Muirhead, Alex Bruce, George Gibson, Graham Brown, John Thomson, the last of worldwide reputation on diseases of children. The last two looked after little Ivy in her last illness and were most kind.

What a crowd! It could not be equalled anywhere else in Britain or America: probably only in Paris, Vienna and Berlin were there comparable crews, though individual brilliant men were to be found in main centres.

Old Sir William Muir, who had been a prominent administrator in India was Principal. In the other faculties there were also famous professors. But that was the last high tide of the University and extra-mural teaching staff in Edinburgh. Medicine was stronger than Surgery: and the men were of higher reputation. It is the other way about since Bruce and Gibson died in 1910: and Bramwell was getting past his best. Medicine though quite good has not produced men of world fame whereas Edinburgh Surgery has been amongst the best in the world for the last 25 or 30 years, with Sir Harold Stiles, Sir David Wilkie (who wrote one of his first papers with me), Henry Wade and Sir John Fraser. Now it can hold its own anywhere: but not so Medicine or Midwifery. Well as I go on I'll be referring again to most of these men, some at greater length than others. But they were almost all my friends; and most of them are away and there have been none to replace them.

Joe Bell was the original of Sherlock Holmes – more of him later. He had a great idea of your mother, and every forenoon used to pass Mayfield Road in his two-horsed Victoria and hoped to see her at the window to wave greeting to her. When she was in for her final professional examination I spoke to him about her and he promised to do his very best for her. We were then engaged.

At his out-patient cliniques (sic) in the Infirmary he used to astonish his students by telling them the occupation of a patient, the road he had come to town and all sorts of things about his life

81

activities all from observation of little things, hands, dress, boots and the kind of mud on them and pretty well diagnosed the complaint before the patient opened his mouth – even although it might be a first visit. Conan Doyle was one of his students and he later developed the character – Sherlock Holmes – from his memory of Joe Bell's feats of observation and deductive reasoning. 'Hullo! Shennan, my boy!' was his usual greeting. He was President of the College of Surgeons in 1889–90 and lived to a great age. His principle for a healthy life was to take a walk of five miles every day.

Heron Watson was a most impressive personality. He had been brought up in the days before anaesthetics when speed in operating was essential to save shock and suffering of the patient. Amputation of the leg in seconds – under a minute; cutting into the bladder and removal of stones in 30 to 35 seconds and so on. When removing the tongue, he would hold the knife blade short and with one sweep cut through the floor of the mouth internal to the lower jaw from one angle to the other – can't draw it, but it was a horse-shoe shaped incision – and just opening all round through the mucus membrane of the mouth. I have not heard of any other who could do it. In the 80s and 90s he had left the Infirmary and was in charge of Chalmer's Hospital – along Lauriston.

When I was a candidate for Conservatorship of the Royal College of Surgeons of Edinburgh Museum, the portly old gentleman came up to the Museum and spent at least an hour learning about my activities – this was about 1900. Dowden, son of Bishop Dowden, was in against me, and I believe it was he who came up to see me after I had been elected and told me I should have been at the meeting of the fellows to hear Heron Watson's powerful advocacy of my claims, which really secured the appointment for me. He had already been President; but was re-elected for the quat-centenary celebrations in 1905 though a very old man – yet regarded as the doyen of the Fellows.

The College was founded in 1505, the same year as King's College here. What a tremendous celebration that was, with a most magnificent dinner in the Music Hall and Assembly Rooms in George Street. The President's Council always meet before Annual Dinners to have a sample dinner with proposed wines. Heron Watson and another old stager, Dunsmure, knew all there was to know about eats and drinks and the wines we had were of the very best superb and each guest had a little box containing two huge cigars wrapped in silver paper – in addition to cigarettes. Some of the guests were very lively afterwards and a bit mixed.

Dr Tommy Thyme protested, for instance, that he knew the President of the Royal College of Physicians by his having a row of snowballs down the front of his robes. But in these days the medical dinners were numerous and good and I was out frequently to them and to other private dinners and dances. Knowing all the prominent medicals brought one in contact with most of the best and nicest people in Edinburgh; one of the things I missed when I came here. Of course all the prominent men nowadays in Edinburgh were either students or very junior members of the staffs of University or Infirmary or Surgeon's Hall School of Medicine.

But Joe Bell and Heron Watson have dragged me off my course and taken me on 13 or more years from where I was speaking of my student days. So I must return to these and continue with Turner and other teachers of Anatomy.

Turner was a native of Lancaster and had come as Assistant to Goodsir away back in the late fifties of last century. Naturally he succeeded Goodsir, as already he had built up a great reputation by his work on the structure of the brain in man and the lower animals.

He was of medium height, stockily and sturdily built, with – to the undergraduate – a grim, stern face and gruff voice which in reproof, in public, could be terrifying. Grizzly-bearded, as usual then, very thin on top and usually wearing a black velvet skull cap. But occasionally he would unbend and could be facetious. 'This bone, gentlemen, is the bone of the upper arm, and is ter-r-med the humerus; some people would say it derives its name from being in propinquity to the "funny bone". There can be no doubt, however, etc. etc.' (Of course, the 'funny bone' is not a bone at all but a nerve at the elbow pressum on which causes 'pins and needles' in the hand and fingers – ring and little finger.) He was sometimes called 'No dubiety', from one of his favourite and frequent expressions.

In my time over 600 students were working in the dissecting rooms; and the number of medical students was over 2000. That number has never been reached since probably chiefly because an Act in 1889 increased the curriculum to 5 years, taking effect from 1895.

He went faithfully through all the bones, muscles, nerves, etc. but when it came to the complicated mass of tiny muscles, etc, in the foot, it was always time for a meeting of the General Medical Council, and take which you like – post hoc or propter hoc – David Hepburn had to lecture on the foot.

You may be sure there were never rows in his class; though away up at the back one or two rebels would spend the hour reading the evening paper or in other ways than listening. After all it was all in the excellent textbook by Gray. I remember well the sequel to some noise or interruption in the back bench, rather to the left of centre of the theatre. I knew perfectly well who was the culprit from my seat near the front on the same side; but Turner stopped, put on his grimmest look, abruptly ceasing to speak about the circulation in the foetus – the unborn babe – and you'll know that a baby at birth and for some days after is of a bright red colour.

He looked up under his heavy, beetling eyebrows and transfixed a poor youth, Taylor, with his gaze for a minute or two. Taylor was one of the mildest, gentlest, most harmless men in the class and of course was completely innocent. But he got redder and redder, as we all (200) turned to look where the Professor was gazing. Then after the poor chap must have felt parboiled Turner remarked very slowly, 'There is a gentleman at the top of the theatre, evidently guilty because he wears a very foetal aspect, as all may see.' Poor innocent Taylor was 'Foetal aspect' ever after, even when he practised in Edinburgh. We were all very sorry that he, by his nervousness, had laid himself open to such a severe reproof while the real culprit, with the usual nerves of steel, sat near him unperturbed and quite enjoying the scene.

Hepburn, after many years as senior assistant went to Cardiff as Professor. Next to him was Robert Howden, a tall smart handsome man, rather like Sir John Marnoch who could make marvellous drawings with coloured chalk on the blackboard. We all liked him and envied his facility in speaking and drawing. He became Professor in the Durham School of Medicine in Newcastle on Tyne. He and his sisters remained to the end faithful patients of Lawson. Then as demonstrators he had Harold Stiles with his terrible stammer which by a strong sustained effort he surmounted, Logan Turner (son of Professor William Turner), Dobie, a son of a doctor in Chester and others.

After I returned to Edinburgh in 1892, I joined the band and I have a large photo of the demonstrators (graduates) of that time in the large portfolio upstairs. Stiles was Professor of Clinical Surgery after Caird and before Wilkie.

I had demonstrated in Anatomy as a senior student and got to know the subject really well. After I had returned after my two years' assistantships in the country, I demonstrated for a year under Turner and then went to help Whittaker in his extra-mural class at Minto House. Later he went to Surgeon's Hall where there was a very good and large dissecting room. As you may surmise a big airy room was needed for such smelly work: in those days the bodies were not so well preserved as nowadays. Turner sent for me to ask why I had left him. I said, I thought I was not an essential member of staff and he replied very kindly that that was not for me to judge. Turner was really a very kind-hearted and considerate man, as all 'big' men are: and I could always go to him for advice and I think he got to like me.

When his portrait by Sir James Guthrie was presented in 1912, Arthur Balfour in the chair, Turner after acknowledging Balfour's remarks, came slowly down the long University Library Hall, while we all stood. He was then 80 years old. I was standing at the back leaning against a pillar but he came out of his way to the door to speak to me. No wonder I hated to leave Edinburgh.

Then in the fight over my position in the Royal Infirmary – Senior Pathologist since 1902. Sheriff Coole and Sir James Affleck represented the Managers of the Infirmary and with Turner, then Principal, were one or two University people. Coole was Lord Justice Clerk and very strong mentally. At a hot part of the discussion, Turner began to shake his forefinger at Coole to emphasise some point and seemed almost at the point of losing his temper. But Coole just waggled his forefinger at Turner and said, 'Now Turner there's no use you shaking your finger at me. I'm not a student,' and the temporary ill-will dissolved in laughter and I still have the letter extending my term of office for a second five years, which would have ended in 1917 or 1918.

Lorrain Smith, who had just become Professor in Edinburgh, wanted to clear me out, so as to have a free hand in the Infirmary in spite of the work I had done for ten years and more in building up the department. For example, I started Clinical Pathology, with WT Ritchie as my Clinical Pathology Assistant, one of the first in the country and also in 1908 introduced the new method of testing the blood for presence of venereal disease – before anyone else in Edinburgh.

I was the first in Britain to demonstrate the organismal cause of syphilis in 1905–6, shortly after it had been discovered by

Schaudinn and Hofmann. I wrote a long paper for the Lancet with illustrations: and was asked up to London to lecture on it – before the Hunterian Society, the lecture being published in a special volume of the Sydenham Society's Transactions along with Schaudinn's & Hofmann's papers.

Lorrain Smith wanted me to go to Kingston, Ontario: but I declined and said I would wait for the result of the Aberdeen Election, which of course went in my favour. At that time I was one of the two best known morbid anatomists in the Kingdom. The other, HM Turnbull, is still at the head of his department at the London Hospital.

After I was appointed to Aberdeen, I wrote to Turner and he sent back his congratulations and good wishes for my future.

In the Senior Anatomy class we had frequent oral exams in the big lecture theatre. Turner went around us showing a specimen and asking what it was. Only those who answered all questions correctly during the whole term were given medals. I was one of the lucky ones. That accurate knowledge of Anatomy proved a great stand by in my later work in Museum and post-mortem room. Though, mind you, had I been asked after graduating what line I should want to take up, Pathology would have been the very last thing to occur to me.

I came into Pathology pretty well by following my nose and doing each new job I was offered as well as I could. It started with being Tutor in Cathcart's ward for women students, then assisting him at operations and in the Surgeons' Museum; then he recommended me to Bruce as assistant, in his class of Pathology and Bacteriology in Surgeons' Hall, meantime keeping up work with Cathcart and doing much of the preparation of the 2nd Volume of the Museum Catalogue; I wrote the 3rd Volume myself.

During this time, i.e. after 1897–8, I met your mother: the first time at a meeting of examiners; when she came to hear the result of her

1st Professional: later when I tutored the ladies in Surgery and bandaging and occasionally coached her in Pathology in the Museum of the Royal College of Surgeons where the romance developed: but such are not things to commit to paper: better tell you by word of mouth. Ergo, to continue.

(Apparent end of letter.)

I should have explained more about those operations I mentioned.

Operations for removal of the tongue are practically all for cancer, started sometimes by the irrigation of a rough tooth or denture or by the heat and irritation from smoking a short stemmed pipe, more in the days of clay pipes than now when the cigarette is the working man's (and woman's) smoke.

Clinical Pathology includes the examination and diagnosis of all sorts of things from patients – tissues, fluids pus (matter), blood, various discharges from all sorts of sources and from most diseases but particularly those of infective origin; but also from diseases due to disordered bodily chemistry or disordered internal secretions which are of a nature similar to the vitamins everyone knows something about nowadays.

Yes, I would be back in the midst of all the activities of the College of Surgeons, if I were back in Edinburgh, but this war puts that further away than ever and I see practically no-one here. However, I keep busy with my hobbies and carpentering.

In physiology – then called Institutes of Medicine – I missed William Rutherford who was off work for a winter session, and in his place J Berry Haycraft lectured. He was a queer chap, hair parted in the middle and brushed down flat on either side and the only, or almost the only teacher who was shaved as to the chin: but he had a longish well cared for moustache, and short side whiskers. He looked a bit lackadaisical and spoke lazily. He was a good teacher but not inspiring. He went later to a chair in Birmingham and Cardiff.

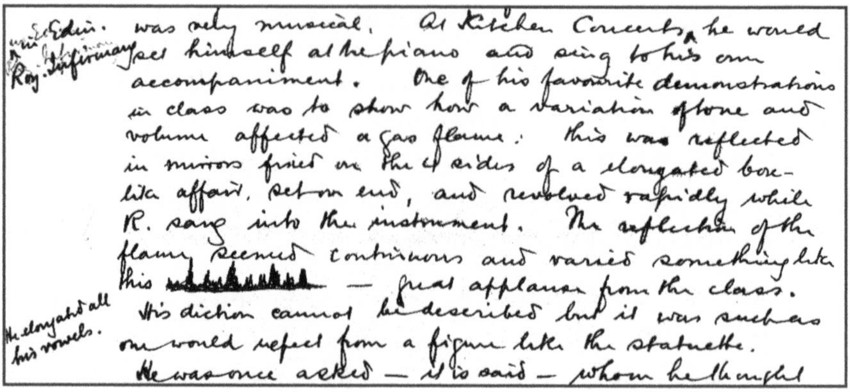

[Handwritten draft at top of page:]

Edin. ...was only musical. At Kitchen Concerts, he would
Roy. Infirmary set himself at the piano and sing to his own
accompaniment. One of his favourite demonstrations
in class was to show how a variation of tone and
volume affected a gas flame. This was reflected
in mirrors fixed on the sides of an elongated box-
like affair, set on end, and revolved rapidly while
R. sang into the instrument. The reflection of the
flame seemed continuous and varied something like
this ——————— great applause from the class.
He elongated all his diction cannot be described but it was such as
his vowels. one would expect from a figure like the statuette.
He was once asked — it is said — whom he thought

It was a great treat to have Rutherford back in the summer session. He was a character, and the little statuette I have of him by WG Stevenson RSA is very like. He had a fine baritone voice and was very musical. At Kitchen Concerts in Edinburgh Royal Infirmary, he would sit himself at the piano and sing to his own accompaniment. One of his favourite demonstrations in class was to show how a variation in tone and volume affected a gas flame: this was reflected in mirrors fixed on the sides of an elongated box-like affair, set on end, and revolved rapidly while Rutherford sang into the instrument. The reflection of the flame seemed continuous and varied, something like this .... – great applause from all the class. His diction cannot be described but it was such as one would expect from a figure like the statuette (he elongated all his vowels).

He was once asked – it is said - whom he thought the greatest physiologist. 'Well, I should say Helmholz is the second.' Indicating that, in joke or earnest, he placed himself first. His eminence in research is indicated by the figure of a rabbit on the base of the statuette. He had done a lot towards explaining the nature of the bile pigments – which are bilirubin (a red one); bilixanthin (yellow); and biliverdin (green) – and he was always referred to by us as bilirubin, partly for this reason and partly because it corresponded pretty well to his name. 'bilirubin' is on the base of his statuette also. He always walked when outside with overcoat buttoned up, gloved hands flat against his thighs, head held well back – with usual top hat – and eyes half closed: but he didn't miss much. In later years at Edinburgh he did less research but spent most of the day carefully preparing his lecture and demonstrations and experiments illustrating it. He was not such a great man intellectually as some of the others, but he was very impressive to his class of 400 or so and had any amount of personality.

I tried hard for a medal in his practical class but was beaten by a sharp Australian – Tucker. It was a case of spotting all the tissues in a series of microscopic sections. He started each answer by putting down 4 to 6 common tissues which are present in almost all organs: whereas I put down things I actually saw under the microscope, which took longer and was more difficult and he came out above me.

Rutherford had an assistant Sutherland, who cut all sections for the class – for each of us to mount on slides. It must have taken up most of his day, during the summer session. He became Professor of Physiology in Columbia University, New York.

His (R's) successor Schafer and one of his assistants, Herring, claimed to have demonstrated tiny bile channels actually within the cells of the liver; but Rutherford had already shown these and the section of liver I still have and which I got in his practical class shows them quite well – I think injected with some coloured fluid. Rather remarkable when you consider that a liver cell is about this size (...) when magnified 300 to 500 times.

Physiology has to do with the normal in structure, in function and in chemical changes in the tissues. Pathology with the abnormal and diseased conditions.

Materia Medica, which at that time had to do solely with drugs of organic (vegetable) or inorganic origin with a little hydrotherapy – treatment by baths – was taught by Professor TR Fraser, later knighted, with a senior assistant, Ralph Stockman, whom you met when Professor in Glasgow: he went there in 1897 or 98 and Robert Muir in 1899. Fraser was also Dean of the Faculty and as such rather held in awe by us. But he was also very dignified, precise and kept himself on the professorial pedestal removed far away from such common mud as students: very reserved, deliberate and rather slow and drawling in speech: but he could occasionally make a very dignified sort of joke, and then he allowed the upper part of his face to relax and his eyes to twinkle. But he walked stiffly too, and altogether took his position and himself seriously. He lectured in a frock coat, often with one hand under a coat-tail and the other elbow resting on his reading desk, his eyes slowly wandering to and fro over his class. He had wards in the Infirmary on the medical side and I clerked in them for part of my attendances. He was a good teacher and strict.

One day a clerk was reading out to us the history of a case. 'Patient has recently become very depressed. He is an undertaker and his low spirits are mainly caused by the non-success of his undertaking.' 'H'm, rather a grim joke,' remarked Tommy Fraser. John Wyllie, an extra-mural physician who was a favourite with the students as he put things so simply and clearly and was not highly regarded by TRF who one day referred to W's teaching, 'Dr Wyllie teaches you that the causes of abdominal distension are Fat, Fluid, Flatus (wind). I would venture to add "Fudge"' – this word spoken very vehemently.

Fraser's fame rested on his separation and identification of the alkaloidal essential principle of the Calabar Bean (the ordeal bean) and its mode of action in the body, making it available for employment in medicine; on his collaboration with Crum Brown to which I have already referred; to his discovery of a remarkable heart stimulant – strophanthus; and on a very extensive investigation of snake venoms – with other things.

Some years after I graduated he was head of a Commission to India which investigated diseases common in that country. Under all his stiffness and dignity he had a very kind heart, as I found to my advantage during the examination (professional) in his subject.

The second professional in those days was abominably and cruelly severe. It comprised four of the heaviest subjects of the course – Anatomy, Physiology, Pathology and Materia Medica - and failure in one brought one down in the lot. The work was overwhelming in scope and in the detail demanded, and to prepare for it I constantly worked right through the night. I lost 2 stones in weight during that awful time.

As a result I suffered from brain-fug: and when I went up for my oral in Materia Medica I could not name a single specimen or answer a question put to me: and I was sent out of the room and passed the rest of the day and the following night in the depths of despair. Luckily I had done a 76% paper and next morning a servitor brought across to Thirlestane Road a note written by Dr Woodhead pathologist, who later founded the Path. Society of Great Britain and Ireland – asking me to come in, in an hour or so – I have still this note – for another oral. I had only time to look up some doses of drugs.

Fraser was there on the other side of the table; and I had evidently been able to have some sleep during the night as I had recovered from my brain-fug and answered correctly all the questions he asked me and named all the specimens he put before me. When it was all over; Fraser asked me what had been wrong the previous day. Had I been nervous? I thought it better to leave it at that and replied – 'I suppose so.'

But by that time I had been recognised as a hard worker; so that that reputation and my good paper saved me. I managed all right with the other three subjects. There was one funny incident in my Pathology oral, however, which may be recalled. Greenfield was very subject to cold and sore throats and when colded was very sorry for himself. At the oral he had one, and was, or made out he was, very much below par. He began asking me questions in a hoarse whisper, and before I could check myself I found myself answering him in a whisper. I at once pulled up: but often thought of it with a chuckle.

The Calabar bean was used by the natives in West Africa in their trials by ordeal. The accused was given one to chew and if it killed him it showed that he was guilty. Now, it is fatal when taken in minute quantities, but when a lot is taken it causes sickness and the vomiting gets rid of the poison and saves the individual. A man who knew he was guilty was afraid to do more than nibble at the bean, whereas the innocent man, conscious of his innocence, ate it freely, with results as above.

In an old purse of Father's which I have there are two labelled Calabar Beans which a missionary brought him from the UP Mission in Old Calabar and exhibited at a church meeting in Bathgate in the seventies [1870s].

Stockman took the practical classes in Mat. Medica and was the sleepiest, or most sleep provoking, lecturer I ever experienced. He sat droning away to us and I regularly went to sleep.

The means used by the more mischievous to keep others awake was to rub furtively the backs of the hands of our neighbours with a brown powder that caused intense itching. I cannot remember its name and I have lost my lecture notes long ago: but it was made up of tiny hairs, like those on the nettle leaf, and those in the interior of the large red dog-hips (of the wild rose). It was used to produce counter-irritation, e.g. like mustard, and is apparently not used now as it does not appear in more recent text books.

Fraser was slight, with thin, hatchet, face: with close clipped beard and moustache, the beard slightly pointed at the chin and dark brown-grizzled. There was a characteristic statuette of him by WG Stevenson and 'Quasi Cursores' gives a pretty fair portrait.

He was another forcible, strong-minded personality and world famous, standing on a basis even better founded that most of his colleagues. Late in life Turner (as Principal) who was I fancy older than he suggested that he ought to retire. Fraser's retort was, 'All right, Turner. I'll retire when you do.' That was the end of that.

His son Francis took my class at Surgeon's Hall and I taught him his pathology & Bacteriology. He is now head of the Medical Unit at the British Post-Graduate School, Hammersmith: where John Gray went as Reader in Morbid Anatomy and whence Aitken came here [Aberdeen] as Professor of Medicine. The latter was Reader (Senior lecturer) under Frank Fraser.

JR Fraser was so spare that he might or may have been the victim of an old chronic tuberculosis: his cheeks were thin and he had often a slight cough, almost like clearing the throat rather than a real cough. He lived in 21 or 22 Drumsheugh Gardens, almost or quite next door to Sir Byrom Bramwell, i.e. on the east side.

Wm Smith Greenfield taught Pathology and he was the most – almost – absurdly conscientious preparer of lectures of the lot. Every thing had to be absolutely up-to-date; and he tried to give us everything about everything, sometimes 6 or 7 theories explaining a thing or a disease and then omitting to give his dogmatic opinion on it, which would have been something to build upon, for we were not qualified to sift the likely from the unlikely of the theories, and the result often was to leave us quite 'in the air'. He was too keen to have everything accurate, and far too self-critical.

Halliday Croom told a story of a consultation he and Halliday had over some patient. After a prolonged and meticulous investigation of the case Greenfield gave about half a dozen possible diagnoses and then left the house, leaving Croom exhausted on a chair in the hall. After a few minutes the bell rang and Croom opened the door to find Greenfield there. 'Oh, Croom, I have just thought of two other possibilities as to diagnosis.' Croom, it is said, said something like 'Good God, Greenfield, Go!!!' and slammed the door in his face.

Greenfield had wards also and everything there had to be exact and up-to-date. It was too much for the most brilliant man possible to keep up-to-date in rapidly growing science like Pathology

and Bacteriology, as well as in Medicine and both suffered. Had he stuck to Pathology and declined the wards, he would have been the greatest pathologist of his age; and had he confined himself to the clinical, he would also have reached the first rank. He made many discoveries long before others made them and reported them; but the trouble was that he would not publish until he was quite sure so that many of his discoveries were not credited to him. I remember once arranging a demonstration for post-graduates in which I showed the organism causing the disease Glanders, in horses and in man. He came round to see what I had and in reference to the glanders organism, he told me, 'You know, Shennan, I saw that in 1874 at least 8 years before it was described, by a German.'

Greenfield was of middle height, clean shaven except for moustache, smooth pink cheeks, spectacled, wore his hair rather long, but carefully brushed down. It was grey when I last saw him. He wore a short frock coat, always buttoned up and a stand-up collar, which looked tight, with a space in front, the sides having sharp points which irked him; rather round back. He was very alert and was than inclined to be sarcastic; so, though admired, for his wide knowledge of everything pathological, bacteriological and medical, he was not beloved as a man.

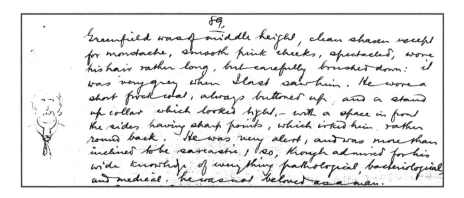

89.

Greenfield was of middle height, clean shaven except for moustache, smooth pink cheeks, spectacled, wore his hair rather long, but carefully brushed down: it was very grey when I last saw him. He wore a short frock coat, always buttoned up, and a stand up collar which looked tight, – with a space in front the sides having sharp points, which irked him, rather round back. He was very alert, and was more than inclined to be sarcastic; so, though admired for his wide knowledge of everything pathological, bacteriological and medical, he was not beloved as a man.

Perhaps there was an innate shyness and a feeling as if people were hostile; which was a great mistake in a man of his mental calibre.

Dr J Hamilton, my predecessor here *(in Aberdeen)*, was assistant to Sanders who preceded Greenfield in Edinburgh, and Hamilton was the best teacher of pathology I have ever known. He really should have got the Edinburgh Chair and was a candidate with Greenfield. But his wife was a curse to him; she drank and together the wives of the Town Councillors – especially of those who at that time represented the City on the Board which elected the professors – made a dead set against Hamilton, and managed to sway the election in Greenfield's favour (1881).

Hamilton while with Hughes Bennett, the Professor of Physiology had initiated the use of the microscope in <u>teaching</u> practically; and this was later extended by Greenfield. I still have somewhere the sections I mounted in his (G's) class.

About the same time (1881–2) Erasmus Wilson, a London skin specialist, left £10000 or so to Aberdeen University to found a Chair of Pathology, and Hamilton was appointed by invitation. All his old pupils I have met spoke of his wonderful teaching, in spite of the lack of material, and the poor museum he had here.

The models he made of various tissues and arrangements of tissues were extraordinarily ingenious, especially one of the tracts along which sensations pass in the spinal marrow up to the brain:

and he invented a machine by which he cut thin sections (microscopic slices) of whole organs which were then mounted between sheets of glass and could be examined under the microscope; especially of the brain of which he had expert knowledge.

My chief, CW Cathcart, invented a mixture of glyceride, glue with – I think – zinc oxide or carbonate, which when set was approximately of the density and had the consistency of skin and tissues and with which he made casts of organs and tissues. These could be coloured up with oil paints closely to resemble the natural appearances.

Hamilton, in addition, was an artist. He painted good pictures; and applying this knowledge to these casts, he produced very life-like – or rather natural-looking appearances. I retained some of the best in the museum I left behind me. I gathered about 3000 good preparations; but doubt if all of them have been kept. I haven't seen the museum since I left.

Every time Hamilton came to Edinburgh, he came to see me at the Infirmary and we had many talks, the older man encouraging the younger to carry on. He died in 1908. He was a good man and his later years were happier, because when his first wife died he married an old sweetheart of his youth, a Miss Wilson – aunt of Henry Wade – who came from Falkirk. Hamilton worked in harmony with MacWilliam here. They shared the microscopes necessary for their practical classes. But there was a regular feud between him and Struthers – Professor of Anatomy – who was disliked by most of his colleagues – another sarcastic divvil (*sic*).

Greenfield's assistants in my time were German Sims Woodhead (GSW against Greenfield's WSG) and a chap Cavlier who must have been of foreign – French or Italian – extraction and who later went to Birmingham. I encountered Woodhead only in the post-mortem room. He wore a short beard, was very handsome and tall and was the first superintendent of the Laboratory of the

Royal College of Physicians, which was first in Lauriston Lane, now absorbed into the Infirmary grounds. Later a very good friend of mine (see later).

That was where I began research on alkaloids and active principles of plants. Diarmid Noel Paton was superintendent at that time. He was the son of the famous artist. He also was very good looking and also wore a short beard. He was blonde and sat as model to his father for his representations of Christ; just as his beautiful sisters acted as models for the beautiful women and angels he painted. He went to Glasgow as Professor of Physiology about the same time as Muir went to the Chair of Pathology there.

There was a third assistant to Greenfield whose name I forget. He taught us most of our microscope work, and I think went abroad later – possibly to Australia.

Greenfield's son (HG?) – he had 12 or 13 of a family – is Pathologist at Queens' Square National Neurological Hospital (that is not the correct name) and he has made a great name for himself in London. When listening to him giving a paper, I was reminded of his father – he has almost all his mannerisms, even to the plucking at his collar in front.

George Duncan, whom you will remember as my first assistant [at Aberdeen], was assistant also in Hamilton's time. He had no ambition to be anything else – too much private income, a bad thing for a young man – and I should have kicked him out when I came here, as he took a lot of work from me and income that I should have had.

At a class dinner, Duncan proposed the health of his chief, Hamilton, and in doing so slyly poked fun at his (Hamilton's) increasing girth. In his reply Hamilton went on quite quietly and then referred to the proposer of the toast. 'When I consider my young friend's present proportions, I shudder to think of the figure he will present, say ten or fifteen years hence.'

99

There are stories galore about Hamilton and I expect each of his old pupils could tell a different one. He had two sons, both of whom went through medicine. When one of them came in for his oral Hamilton, in his gruffest voice, asked, 'What is your name, sir?' 'Hamilton.' 'Ah – first name?' 'So and so.' He treated them just like the other students.

He had a favourite tuberculosis sputum spit from a consumptive patient – which was alive with the organisms of the disease and which he had used in successive classes. As he walked up and down in front of the class he explained, or rather bellowed, just how very good for the purpose this sputum was and how every member of the class would be sure to demonstrate the organisms – after staining – under the microscope. Meantime he had sent his attendant – Rae – for the bottle of sputum, but the latter had let it fall on to the floor and most of the contents were lost. So he was engaged feverishly spitting and spitting into the bottle to make up the contents to what Hamilton knew should be there. The results were distinctly disappointing to Hamilton, as man after man produced preparations which showed 'not a tail': and he did not know what to make of the failure. I did not hear if ever the cause of the failure was explained to him. This was a Bulloch story.

Chapter IV in 'Arches of the Years' by Halliday Sutherland, gives a very good first hand word-picture of Hamilton (at about 1905), which would be worth your while reading as it pictures a really strong character who feared no man and yet was at heart the kindest ever.

It was a privilege to call him friend and to know that he had some very kind regard for me. A few years before his death at the age of 59, though he looked 70, he was made a Fellow of the Royal Society of London for his work on disease in the sheep. His nickname was 'The Bull'.

I shouldn't wonder if Dr Agnes Thomson had been in the same class as Halliday Sutherland. No, in the next year class.

He (HS) indicates towards the end of that chapter that Greenfield became blind before he died; but I think that is a mistake. He certainly became very depressed and morose – almost mental – and his death must have been a relief to himself as to his family. He had a house in Heriot Row but had rooms for study in India Street, round the corner. One can hardly work with a family of a baker's dozen wandering round all the time.

Of course in those days rents and other costs were 1/2 to 1/3 of what they now are [1940].

Robert Muir graduated 2 years before me and was Greenfield's assistant till he went to Dundee in 1898 passing to Glasgow the following year.

Greenfield's work and experience in Pathology have not received the recognition they deserved; and wherever I could, in my own book, I pointed out where he had done pioneer work: though the credit had been claimed by others.

He was a riling chap, though. When I was Senior Pathologist in Edinburgh Royal Infirmary, I had to take off some fluid from the spinal canal – which encloses the spinal marrow – for examination. It is a rather difficult and ticklish job, as one has to calculate the exact position to go in, so as to pass the long hollow needle through a narrow space between the vertebrae and avoid injuring the spinal marrow. He came and watched me, and though his critical and sarcastic presence rather put the wind up on me, I went in first shot and without greatly disturbing the patient.

Once I discussed a point with him in one of my researches and I got little out of him except, 'Well, Shennan, I wish you joy of your work,' on whatever it was. I took him out several times in consultation over cases when I was in practice in Edinburgh, and the last time he so riled me that I felt, 'Well, you sarcastic old b., I'll not have you out again.' I once took a curious kidney to him, and was pleased to find that he knew no more about the condition than I did, or at least said so. He knew more about kidney diseases than anyone else.

A few years ago I was talking during a Varsity Reception with Dr David Lawson who ran the Sanatorium at Banchory and now bosses Ruthin Castle Sanatorium in North Wales. I was speaking about Dr Alex Bruce and the time when I was his assistant in Pathology at Surgeon's Hall, particularly instancing one year when Bruce was Co-examiner in the University and at one exam Greenfield had ploughed his (B's) medallist, and in revenge Bruce ploughed Greenfield's. Lawson said, 'Well, that's interesting; I happened to be Bruce's (or Greenfield's) medallist who was spun.'

Greenfield had something womanish about him which made him do spiteful things like that.

He was his own worst enemy: he was too damned critical not only of others' but of his own work, and did not publish till he was absolutely sure he was correct. That is why he did not put on record all of his discoveries as soon as they were made. At the end of his life he was far in front of his contemporaries with regard to the pathology of Inflammation of the Lung; but was collecting the histories and post-mortem accounts of cases and wanted to have 1000 before publishing his results. Of course he never got his 1000; and all those observations, records and specimens have gone for nothing. No one else could have used them and his notes on every case were most voluminous. In my book I give him credit for discovering the part of the lung where the inflammation begins, a thing which had been claimed recently by some young whipper-snapper.

He was English and was on the staff of St Thomas's Hospital and some other London Hospitals and later was Professor at the Brown Institute there before going to Edinburgh.

As a clinician he was extraordinarily good at diagnosis and was often proved most accurate if the case came to post-mortem examination.

102

Sims Woodhead was such a success as Superintendent of the RCP Laboratory in Edinburgh, that he was asked to set up a similar laboratory in London on the Embankment, for the Colleges of Surgeons and Physicians there conjointly. He was a good friend and always ready to advise on and criticize my work.

Later he became Professor at Cambridge, where he died. His family was connected with some important factories from which he had an independent income. He was the founder – with Hamilton chiefly – of the Pathological Society of Great Britain and Ireland, and first editor of its Journal, in which most of my own best work has appeared – apart from that I embodied in my book.

The site of the conjoint laboratory on the Embankment was absorbed by the Hotel Cecil or Savoy, and the laboratory became the Jenner Institute in Great Russell Street next to the British Museum on its west side. Later it became the Lister Institute which you know about and of which the superintendent is now Sir John Ledingham, an old pupil of Hamilton's. Professor Wm Bulloch and Sir Arthur Keith to whom I gave you an introduction when you went to London were also old enthusiastic disciples.

Next I come to the Final Exam subjects, Surgery, Medicine and Midwifery and I have quite a lot to tell about the various teachers and their little ways.

John Chiene was the Prof of Systematic Surgery and Thomas Arrandale of Clinical Surgery. They had both been under the great Lister when he was in Edinburgh before he went to London to convince the rather pig-headed surgeons there – some of them of world-wide fame – of the efficacy of his antiseptic system, which has saved many millions of lives throughout the world. Incidentally the first to see its importance was a Danish Surgeon, Saxtorph.

Chiene was nicknamed 'Honest John' because he seemed so forthright; but he had his distinct weaknesses. Robert Muir couldn't stand him. He used to play golf with him against Argyll Robertson (the eye specialist) and I think John Duncan. He once said to Robert on the putting green, when their opponents had a difficult putt for the hole, 'Robert, you'll see I'll make Argyll miss that putt.' And he did so by moving and making some remark just when Argyll was putting: (an unpardonable sin in Robert's eyes, who has always been a stickler for playing the game cleanly and defeating your opponent fairly if you can – a real sportsman).

One day in the Royal Infirmary, Cathcart and Chiene both had a patient die on the operating table while under the anaesthetic. Cathcart was greatly distressed, but put on his coat and told his resident he would go himself to see the waiting friends, explain what had happened and comfort them if possible. Chiene hurriedly washed his hands, put on his coat, and said to the resident 'Well, I'm away out of the Infirmary as fast as I can: you'll have to do the best you can with the friends about explaining the fatality.' And in this cowardly fashion left him to do the best he could: yet I believe this was the first time in our 20000 chloroform anaesthesias he had had a death due to chloroform.

Another time I was operating the steam spray which covered the field of operation with a fine cloud of steam impregnated with carbolic acid. The operation was for the removal of a growth in the neck. The knife went into the jugular vein and there was a flood of blood. Chiene lost his nerve and Caird, who was then his assistant – short-sighted though he was – at once grappled with the situation, secured the open vein and saved that patient's life. The great danger was that air should be drawn in through the vein to the right side of the heart, be churned up with the blood, producing a spongy frothy mass which could not be propelled further into the lung, and the heart would stop beating.

But Chiene was a good dogmatic teacher who just failed at being a <u>great</u> teacher. He used picturesque language and illustration in driving home points in the lecture room and in the wards. 'Now,

Shennan, whit is it a've done wrong? Did ye see, and dae ye understand now whit a should have done!' He was a Fifer and spoke rather broadly. I liked his lectures and did all my surgery in his wards. I used to spend all my evenings in the side rooms writing for and helping with cases and getting all I could out of the successive residents. It was most interesting.

Chiene was keen on Marcus Aurelius in my first year with him and used to quote his writings and aphorisms; or would quote chapter and verse from the Bible. One of my contemporaries, a chap Orr, son of a Professor in the UP Theological College was a casual, careless chap, who would not take pains. Chiene once at the bedside said to him, 'Mr Orr, you're just a Gallio.' Orr was mystified and said he did not understand. 'Juist read The Acts of the Apostles, Chapter 18 and so, verse 17, where you will read "and Gallio cared for none of these things." Yes, Mr Orr, you're juist a Gallio.'

Another day I heard him give a half-caste, Robertson, I think was his name, this terrible dressing down. Robertson was clerk of a case to which he had given chloroform, at the operation. This was on a Saturday, and this scene I am describing, took place at the Monday clinic. We attended every Sunday at some time of the day: though I believe I never missed once or even twice at Kirk, in spite of it.

(Here listened to Roosevelt's broadcast about Italy, 12.15 a.m., 11.6.1940.)

Going round the ward as usual, Chiene came to the case and asked who was the clerk of the case. Robertson said he was. 'Mr Robertson, you gave this poor wumman chloroform on Saturday, didn't ye?' 'Yes Sir.' 'An' why did ye not come up yesterday to see how she was?' 'Well, sir, I was tired, and thought I was entitled to have a rest and a day off like other people.' 'Oh, indeed! Mr Robertson. You know very well, don't you, that it is one of my rules that must not be broken, that when one of my clerks gives a patient an anaesthetic he must come up the next day to ask how she is getting on and to satisfy himself that all goes well.'

'Mr Robertson, when you come to die and appear before the Angel Gabriel and want to enter heaven: he will turn up your name and record in his books, and he'll say to you. "Ah, yes, Mr Robertson, do you remember that poor wumman you chloroformed in Ward XII – Dr Chiene's - of the Edinburgh Royal Infirmary on so-and-so (giving the date and year)?' And, Mr Robertson, you have to say "Yes, ah do." Then Gabriel will say to you, "You know that that poor wumman was seriously ill and you knew Mr Chiene's rule about visiting her the next day, even if it wis a Sunday," and you will have to reply that you did. "An', why didn't ye do what ye knew was your duty?" An' ye'll have nothing to answer. Then do you know what the Angel Gabriel will do next? He will call for Peter, who keeps the gate of heaven and will say to him "Show this gentleman downstairs."'

I've never heard a more devastating reproof. Marcus Aurelius was one of the best of the Roman Emperors – during the 2nd Century AD – and was a philosopher. He wrote his Meditations, the spirit of which comes wonderfully near the heart and conscience of modern Christians.

Later Chiene went in strongly for the writings of a Chinese philosopher which he quoted extensively. I forget the name but will give it if it recurs to memory. Perhaps it was Lao Tzu.

Lawson [Theo's brother] also attended his wards either then or later; and one evening was so overcome by the sight of a case of tetanus or lockjaw that he fainted; and a wee nurse actually hauled him by the shoulders out of the ward. She would weigh about 2/3 of his weight. Luckily there is now a curative serum for such cases and they are now very rare.

During the long summer vacations I spent most of my time in the wards. Chiene would be away and Caird in charge. He was very good, a grand little chap, and frequently made watercolour sketches of his cases, especially the abdominal ones. One summer he had a terribly anxious time, case after case went septic and died, do what he could. He was horribly worried and used to unburden himself to me who gave him what sympathy I could. We always remained good friends.

His sketching may have put me on to an idea. A young woman came in with a bad burn over the buttocks, and Chiene got quite enthusiastic describing the gradual healing of the huge wound and one day he told the class he would give £10 to any artist who could paint the case. I thought I would try it and painted in watercolours the wound at three stages to healing and made a very good job of it. I mounted up the drawings together and took the result in to him. He was awfully pleased, but said, 'Well, Shennan, of course I can't give you the £10: but I'll tell you what I'll do. I'll tell Gardner the instrument maker to give you its value.' So I got the best pocket instrument case of Russian leather with instruments with ivory handles and also a set of knives in box with 'T. Shennan from J. Chiene' engraved on the metal labels. The pictures hung in his museum for years. Last year I looked in the museum, now Dr John Fraser's, but could not see them. They have no doubt been put aside in drawer or cupboard. I don't think, with my name on them, that they would be destroyed.

When I was assistant Conservator to Cathcart in the Museum of the Royal College of Surgeons of Edinburgh, and later when Conservator, I made a considerable number of these casts and painted them. When I was Assistant to Dr Spalding at Gorebridge I noticed that the housemaid – Nellie – had a curious deformed hand.

Ten years later I remembered this and ferreted out the case. It had been a vascular tumour of the hand between the thumb and fingers in infancy and I found out through Mr Hodsdon one of the surgeons to the Infirmary that he had inherited casts of the infant hand (before and after treatment by electricity) from his former chief John Duncan, one of the first cases treated in this way. I copied these casts in Plaster of Paris and got the girl who was then in service in Edinburgh to come up to the Museum, and after several vain attempts, managed to get a good mould of the hand and wrist. I made a cast in Cathcart's material and coloured it up exactly like nature, every wrinkle showing and even a recent insect bite on the back of the hand.

Some time later, taking some ladies round during a reception in the College Hall and museum, I showed them this cast, and they were horrified, thinking it was real. It is still in the Museum along with the two casts of the infant hand – thirty years separating the infant and the adult hands. I often wonder what has become of that girl. She was a splendid girl and very warm-hearted. At Gorebridge the usual supper would be kippers and tea, but I used to stay out late on my rounds and then Nellie brought me to my room a hot supper, usually of mince and coffee which was much more pleasant. I liked that lassie all right. She was a prize brick.

(End of letter.)

18th June 1940

I may as well continue in spite of the – at present – bad war news, for which we have to a great extent to thank our leading politicians of the last 10 years – especially Ramsay MacDonald – and the mistakes made by the French Generalissimos, under whose direction our fellows have done their very best, better than any other troops in the world could have done.

I have mentioned John Duncan, the surgeon. He was a fine upstanding man, with a long spreading beard and a hearty guffaw of a laugh. He was a great golfer, and it was John Duncan's 'Law' that when looking for your ball, you should search 40 yards behind where you thought you reached – and a very good law, too. As a surgeon I did not see much of him. He was one of the extra-mural, good men and in surgery I stuck to the Varsity teachers.

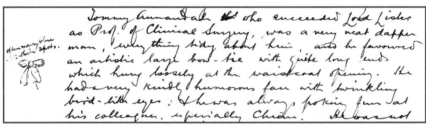

Tommy Annandale who succeeded Lord Lister as Professor of Clinical Surgery, was a very neat dapper man, everything tidy about him and he favoured an artistic large bow-tie with quite long ends which hung loosely at the waistcoat opening. He had a very kindly, humorous face with twinkling bird-like eyes: and he was always poking fun at his colleagues, especially Chiene. He was not so particular as to antiseptics but was very expert with the knife, cutting cleanly – no niggling dissections with tearing up or bruising of the tissues which always leads to trouble, lowering their vitality and making them more prone to sepsis. Hence his results were quite as good, if not better, than those more careful antiseptically. I have actually seen him using a knife picked up from the floor, and blowing through a catheter before drawing off urine.

This was jokingly referred to as Tommy's antiseptic breath. He had a rather sad home life; he married one of the Nelsons, the publisher's, daughters – a lovely blonde plump woman who used to run off on the loose with all sorts and conditions of men. She was not really right mentally: but I think Tommy in the end died of a broken heart.

Mrs Annandale, Mrs Argyll Robertson and Mrs Berry Hunt were the leaders of the smart set in Edinburgh. They were known as The World, The Flesh and the Devil. Mrs A was the Flesh, naturally enough. You can fit up the other two any way you like. They were all fine-looking women and superb in evening dress. I doubt if any of them produced a child – and I think I needn't enlarge further. Argyll Robertson and his wife went to visit some grand Indian Rajah – and many were the suggestions, but AR died there – not the right end for such a fine-looking, famous man, and proud gentleman of the highest breed.

His portrait, in court dress – black velvet – is in the Library of the Royal College of Surgeons, Edinburgh. He was the soul of kindness with patients and had a most delicate touch!

The Professor of Systematic Medicine was Thomas Grainger Stewart – a big rather stout pompous man whose ambition – well known to all, even students – was to be Queen's Physician and a knight. Pears, the soap people, had an advertisement showing a baby in his bath reaching over the side for a cake of soap on the floor. A poster of this was drawn by someone for a Kitchen Concert with Grainger's head and the soap was inscribed 'Knighthood'. He was just a bit of a snob and his children were insufferable. He had done some good work in kidney disease when a young man and to my knowledge never did anything more except run a very profitable consulting practice.

I had several contacts with him – the first at my oral in medicine. He met me, shook hands and started, 'Ah, Mr Shennan, I think I have had the pleasure of writing your father, I think it was at

Aix-les-Bains.' The absurdity of a man with never more than £180 a year or so, with a family of nine, indulging in trips to Aix-les-Bains, was irresistibly funny; but as he did not pursue the subject and let it drop like a hot potato and we got on with a very easy oral. I had no trouble with any of my final subjects; 13 exams and all dead easy. Or so they seemed – I must have known my work pretty well. Grainger's head was rather like your grandfather Green's, with short beard and moustache. He did get his knighthood and was Queen's Physician before he died.

Some years later, I had him out on consultation over a rather important patient in Gorebridge. After the consultation he confirmed all my conclusions and suggested a 'very slight' alteration in the prescription. I must say he was a good consultant. We had a cup of tea later in the drawing room and the patient's nephew, rather far in liquor, was there and had not the respect due to such an eminent consultant. He asked G Stewart while the latter was receiving his cup of tea from the patient's sister, 'Which do you prefer, Sir Thomas, to be called Professor or Doctor?' 'Oh, Professor, I think.' 'Then, I suppose the Doctor here,' pointing to me, 'is one of the small fry.' At that G Stewart backed to sit down, but the big man got only the corner of the chair and nearly slipped on to the floor. It was all so ridiculous, that it was really painful to keep one's face straight.

Now I come to Midwifery and Diseases of Children. The Professor was Alexander Russell Simpson, a nephew of Sir James Y. Simpson, who introduced chloroform as an anaesthetic, and fought tooth and nail for years against denial and lay prejudice. These claimed that it was a Biblical Law that women should bring forth in pain and suffering, and that it was working against Providence to ease their sufferings in this way. He prevailed and Queen Victoria, by insisting on having this anaesthetic with her children, set the seal on his great work. No doubt he was a bit of a showman and advertiser but he was in demand all over the country and worked himself into an earlier grave than necessary:

but all the same he is one of the immortals. Alexander was extremely able, as brainy in his own way as his uncle, but was overshadowed by him. In his lectures he was constantly referring 'to my uncle'.

He was a rather little man with a slight body and a big head. He wore his hair long and had bushy side whiskers, but clean shaven mouth and chin – much the same as my father who, however, kept his whiskers trimmed. As you see him in the very accurate statuette I have (by WG Stevenson RSA) he had a shortish neck, wore a short frock coat, the lapels rather loose, round-lensed pince-nez on a ribbon falling on his coat lapels, rather tight trousers. When he lectured he kept his hands open in front of the body, the thumbs and fingers touching at the hips and raised himself upon his tip-toes to emphasise any point – as shown in the statuette – and occasionally turning his head to one or other side all of a piece with the upper part of his trunk.

He was nicknamed 'Grannie Simpson': but was quite liked, almost loved, by his students. He used to invite them to his house, 52 Queen St (formerly his uncle's), for breakfast or dinner and treated them sumptuously, though took very little alcohol himself. Generally the proceedings included a religious service: for he was deeply and sincerely religious, more so than most of his colleagues: and he was honoured accordingly for all recognised that he practised what he preached most consistently.

His wife was a Barbour of Bonsheid, Perthshire, whose forebears made their money out of the stone trade, and they were all intensely religious, going over the score at times. She used to write little religious books and one of these, Friends and Friendship, was given out to each one of my class. One morning one of these booklets came flying down from the back bench on to the lecture table before Simpson. That was the only time I ever saw him really angry – and he had reason for it.

She must have been a bit of a trial to him and on occasion he had to be very firm with her. She was hypochondriac, imagined herself an invalid and so on.

At our breakfast, a student going in for his Final was invited and in the course of it as usual Mrs S improved the occasion by asking him what his chief purpose in life was. Very naturally he replied that it was to pass his exam. 'A very poor and uninspiring purpose, Sir,' remarked Mrs S and turning to her (then) young son George asked him, 'George, tell the gentleman what your chief purpose in life is!' 'To save souls, Mother, pass the jam!!'

George is about my age and now a town councillor, possibly a future Lord Provost, with a very fine palate for good liquor: and a ruby nose which is not alcoholic but gastric.

On another occasion when the distribution of one of his wife's booklets coincided with a new arrival in his family, he received a great ovation on coming into the lecture theatre. 'Oh, gentlemen, gentlemen you must please realise that it has been my wife's work altogether and solely, I had nothing whatever to do with it.' Of course, the class applied this protest to the wrong subject and great was the hilarity. He was a dear old chap, who liked me and your mother. In the black-out of the last war he was run down by a taxi cab and taken to the Infirmary where he died without regaining consciousness. Poor old chap!

In addition to Simpson's class I took out a summer course with Halliday Croom who lectured at Minto House, Chambers Street; and who later succeeded Simpson in the university chair, which Simpson's brother-in-law Freeland Barbour became lecturer on Diseases of Women. Croom, as I think I have already told you, was the son of the UP Minister of Lauriston Place Church – almost next door to the convent and nearly opposite the upper end of Lady Lawson Street.

> *Lecture on Diseases of Women. Groom, as I think I have already told you, was the son of the U.P. Minister of Lauriston Place Ch. — almost next door to the Convent & nearly opposite the upper end of Lady Lawson St. He was a great dandy; hair glossy and curly, short beard carefully trimmed, clothes just right. — Wide-brimmed silk hat, set slightly to one side, stand up collar open in front, with sharp points — must have been rather uncomfortable. — He was said to bathe & change all his clothes frequently every day. — He wore a long frock coat, the tails always flying out a bit; carefully pressed rather tight trousers, without a crease or fold in them. He lectured in an evening dress cut away coat with tails. He was a very humorous*

He was a great dandy, hair glossy and curly, short beard carefully trimmed, clothes just right. Wide-brimmed silk hat, set slightly to one side, stand-up collar open in front, with sharp points – must have been rather uncomfortable – he was said to bathe and change all his clothes frequently every day. He wore a long frock coat, the tails always flying out a bit; carefully pressed rather light trousers, without a crease or fold in them. He lectured in an evening dress cut away coat with tails. He was a very humorous lecturer and easy to listen to. Almost all the men took out his class as well as Simpson's.

His stories illustrating cases were good, but I recollect clearly only one of them. He was lecturing on Maternal Impressions and their influence on the off-spring: and rather scoffing at the idea as a whole. He spoke rather quickly and tended to run words together. 'Gentlemen – I can give you an example of the influence of maternal impressions. A woman well advanced in pregnancy was passing along a street in Portsmouth near the dockyards, and she came on two seamen fighting and both had wooden legs. They fought and fought until they both fell to the ground with their wooden legs sticking in the air. The poor woman was so over come at the sight that she fainted. Kind neighbours conveyed her to her home where she was presently delivered of a fine male child, who not only had a wooden leg, but a fine brass ferule at the end of it. That, gentlemen, is what I think of the influence of maternal impressions.'

Like all the others, he was very friendly and often brought things from his patients up to use in the Infirmary for examination and report, but though he was making a large income, I never got a penny for any of them. He would say, 'You know, Shennan, I don't know what the clinicians would do without you, your reports are most helpful.' I had not yet the seniority to retort that a fee of 2 or 3 guineas would meet the difficulty.

He, with all, had his own troubles. He told me once about a patient of his, a daughter of Lord ———, whom he had assisted at birth of her infant. The exit parts had been torn slightly, but not enough to give the lady any discomfort and Croom advised him to leave well alone, and not worry having a repair done.

Later she consulted a London man about something else, and in the course of examination he discovered the slight tear and insisted on repairing it in his expensive nursing home – getting a very fat fee for it all. The father, Lord ———, was furious with Croom and sent for him for allowing his daughter to go about without himself having done the repair. Croom explained and wrote the London man to state his reasons for operating. This chap wrote back that he quite recognised that an operation was not essential and could have done without, but this was a chance of a rich patient and a fat fee and ended 'Mais il faut vivre.'

Many London consultants were and still are quite conscious-less about such things: and at that time one felt that an honest opinion could not be obtained south of Leeds.

Another instance was told me by Joseph Montague Cotterill, a surgeon – his father had been Bishop of Edinburgh. A patient of his had taken his young son to a Harley Street surgeon who discovered a blocked duct of the salivary gland under the tongue forming a small transparent sausage-shaped bleb on the floor of the mouth. 'This is a very serious condition and must be operated on at once. I shall ring up Sir ——, and arrange for the boy to have a bed in his nursing home (£15-20 a week).'

The father demurred to this and declined to agree to anything until he had talked it over with his wife. She was a sensible creature and said, 'Well if anything is to be done it will be done in Edinburgh. Fix up some tickets and we'll go off by the next train' which they did. The London man sent them wires to Grantham and York saying they were imperilling the life of their boy, for there was no surgeon in Scotland capable of tackling the case successfully. On arriving home they took the boy to Cotterill who listened to their tale, examined the boy and said, 'So there's no surgeon capable of operating in such an important case. Well, you just wait a moment.' He took a small silver probe, passed it into the duct, released the obstruction and the clear bleb collapsed. Cure in about 2 seconds.

Many similar stories were current and the greedy London consultant had himself to thank.

Meta Hay (now Mrs Dobbie) – was nearly caught. When in London she had an attack of acute tonsillitis and called in a London man, I am ashamed to say an Aberdeen graduate. On his second visit he announced, 'I just happened to meet Dr so-and-so, an Ear and Throat specialist and asked him to see Professor Matthew Hay's daughter with me.' Well he examined the throat and advised strongly that she should go into a nursing home and have the tonsils removed - a mad suggestion in any case in the acutely inflamed condition.

Meta, however, though very seedy was wide awake and said very decidedly, 'Well if my tonsils have to be removed, Henry Peterkin will do it in Aberdeen and no one else.' Seedy though she was, she got on the train and managed home all right. 2 or 3 months later after the inflammation had subsided, the tonsils were safely removed.

116

There was another very funny story about Sir John Halliday Croom. His policy was to make every patient feel convinced that she was the most important patient on his list. That's what makes success as a woman's doctor, especially in the so-called upper classes. In the West End one day he was accosted by a very fine, well-dressed, stylish young woman. He walked along Princes Street talking with animation, and trying all the time to recall the lady's name – but without success. A day or two later a friend tackled him. 'Look here, Croom, what do you mean by parading Princes Street with a woman of that kind?' 'Why she has been a patient of mine. I am sure.' 'Stuff and nonsense, she's one of the most notorious ladies of pleasure in this town.' Croom was not allowed to forget that incident in a hurry.

Then there was Francis Haultain who looked after your mother and once brought his son, at about 7 or 8. When asked what he was going to be, this youngster said he was going to be a doctor but would marry a lady doctor and make her do the work. Later he was here [Aberdeen] as assistant to McKerron for several years and then returned to Edinburgh where he is now one of the foremost midwifery men. McKerron was continually on the phone to Hamilton senior during the trouble when Edward [Theo's second son] was brought into the world.

He was a great golfer and had a pretty and lively wit. He had a story for everything. The only one I remember was of a boat going into Oban bay in a fog, and hailing a yacht, the Helvetia. 'Who are you?' 'Ta Helvicha.' 'To Hell with yourself,' was the response.

Then there were Nathanial Brewis and Haig Ferguson, also in the same line. I worked a good deal with Brewis and had some good cases with him. He was a powerful man; had played rugby in his youth and was a great golfer also. He said he played golf to strengthen the muscles in his arms as that he could lift his patients better.

117

One of our cases was a daughter of the late Earl of Elgin who died with a very acute inflammation of the kidneys. Haig Ferguson had that house in Coates Crescent (No 9) on the side next Princes Street with the extra built-on storey – a private nursing home. He was President of one of the colleges in his time – the Surgeons. He was a good but not outstanding man and had a slight stammer. But a decent sort.

How writing these memoirs brings up before the mind's eye all these men, now passed over, who were all good friends of mine. You cannot wonder that I never felt at home in Aberdeen, and have always hankered after dear old Edinburgh, 'my ain toon'.

After I had been assisting Cathcart for a year or two (1894–95) in private and in the Royal College of Surgeons' Museum, he and Gulland recommended me as Assistant to Dr Alex Bruce, the Lecturer on Pathology at Surgeons' Hall School of Medicine: and that was my introduction to the teaching of Pathology. I kept going also with Cathcart. I had chiefly the practical classes in Pathology, and what, at that time, we could teach, with ordinary (no extra high powers available) microscopes etc. of Bacteriology. To get up the latter I spent a summer vacation at the Jenner Institute in Great Russell Street, and brought back a whole collection of cultures and microscopic preparations: so that I believe I was really teaching Bacteriology before the Varsity people. As Allan McFadyen, the superintendent of the Institute gave out, 'Shennan brought a small hand bag and is taking back several trunks and a suitcase full of our stuff.'

I took over the Lectureship in 1899 when Bruce gave it up on becoming full Physician to the Royal Infirmary. He was extremely able: he had taken his MA at Aberdeen but came to Edinburgh for his medical course. His uncle was proprietor of the estate Inverquhomery, near Longside, and he was left the life-rent of this property. His youngest (?) son is now proprietor. Bruce died 1910–11 of some very obscure complaint, the nature of which was never properly elucidated. He often said to me that for his family's sake a man should always insist on a post-mortem examination but this was not done in his own case.

In his medical course he won almost all the medals and big money prizes available: just as, a little later, Stiles (later Sir Harold Stiles of the Clinical Surgery Chair after Caird) did the same: both winning £1600–£1700 worth of bursaries etc. Bruce was especially good in the anatomy, physiology and pathology of the central nervous system. He was very good to me, and left me all his teaching material – very generous. He had a big house (7? Moray Place, about 7 or 8 storeys) and I was frequently there.

His second daughter, Lydia (?) was a lovely girl, with Titian auburn hair and a perfect complexion, hazel eyes, bright pink lips. She married a Mr Gray and lived or still lives near Peterhead.

Bruce was a tidy well-documented person with a very well arranged mind: and a pawky humour; he could make a joke with a solemn face and then the ends of his lips would gradually rise into a knowing grin, as he looked from under his eyebrows at his listeners. He could tell a good tale too. His favourites were about Pirrie, the Professor of Surgery in Aberdeen prior to Ogston, who was one of the senior surgeons along with him (Pirrie) in the Aberdeen Infirmary: but they were not great friends; in fact Ogston had rather a low opinion of Pirrie. Pirrie had spent some time in Paris with Baron Dupuytren, one of the foremost French surgeons: and after he returned he remained so full of Dupuytren that he became known as Baron Pirrie or 'The Baron'. He was a bit liable to spoonerisisms. For example, trying to open a conversation with Ogston he would say 'Oh! O-o-gston! (he had a stutter) hive ye seen ma hoarse an' pair o' broon kerridges.'

His special story, however, was about a Surgical Clinic in which Pirrie was examining outpatients. 'A man came in. "Weel, ma mannie, whit's the matter wi you?" "It's the utch." "Ah, the itch. Most interesting, gentlemen. Now come round in a nice square circle, an' I'll demonstrate this condition tae ye. Noo, ye see how it has attacked the delicate skin atween the fingers and in the front of the wrist. Ye'll see these long narrow streaks in the skin, wi' wee black spots in them. These are ca'd the burries (burrows) and the spots are the insects that hae burried into the skin. Noo, I'll pass a wee needle along one o' the burries, and when I tak' it out, ye'll see a wee thing attached tae its end, juist a tiny wee spot. That's the insect, the 'acarus', it's ca'd. Very interesting, the 'itch insect'. The disease has ither names, for example the 'baker's itch'." Then an idea struck him and in a rather worried tone he asked, "Whit's yer work, ma mannie?" "I'm a baker." Bruce, quite agitated, "An' whaur dae ye work?" "At Kennaways." Striking his brow with his hand, Pirrie ejaculated "Goad o' my faithers, he bakes ma breed.'" General collapse.

Pirrie was not a great surgeon and did nothing noteworthy. Ogston, on the other hand, carried out most important researches on the causes of suppuration and was the first to demonstrate the rounded microbes – cocci, from 'coccus' a berry which are the chief causes of suppuration and inflammation. He found then in grape-like clusters and in chains. He consulted old Geddes, Professor of Greek, later principal – who suggested 'staphulon', Greek for grape cluster, and 'strepton', a chain. And these pus microbes have been known all over the world ever since as staphylococci and streptococci. The latter are the more virulent and dangerous to life; but recently a chemical substance has been discovered which kills most kinds of them in the blood and tissues.

Sir Alex. Ogston's father, Francis Ogston, was the lecturer in Forensic Medicine before Matthew Hay.

Alex. Ogston was a big man, mentally and physically. I never knew him well and met him only occasionally after he had retired to be succeeded by Marnoch.

Marnoch was full of tales about him. He was rugged, unyielding, liking and liked by some, disliking and disliked by others, including some of his colleagues; Struthers, for example, and his (the latter's) successor Bobby Reid of the Anatomy Chair. Struthers was a bit of a Paul Pry and Nosey-parker.

One day, during the final Professional exams, when crossing the quadrangle of Marischal College, he saw that students were communicating by the deaf and dumb alphabet with others in the Surgery Museum, which you will remember was my department, and getting information as to the questions which were being asked in the Orals. 'Boothie', the attendant who looked after Surgery, Medicine and Midwifery, was near and Struthers told him to tell Ogston what was going on. He did so and Ogston with his slow incisive speech said, 'Booth, will you go and give Professor Struthers my compliments and tell him he can go to Hell.' A short time afterwards he asked, 'Booth, have you given Dr Struthers my message?' 'No, Sir, I have been very busy and haven't had the time.' 'Very well, Booth, you can just tell him at your leisure.'

He liked a story against himself of a sharp riposte from a country yokel. He had been caught far from home in I think a shower and thankfully accepted a lift in a cart. He noticed that the man managed his beast very skilfully and remarked, 'My man, you are quite an adept' – the man took this unknown term as not altogether complimentary and replied, 'You're anither, and a buggar forbye.'

But this has taken me a very long way from Bruce. But since I am stuck for the present for want of Dr deCarl Woodcock's book about Edinburgh doctors of my time, I may break off to tell you about a rather exceptional patient of mine, Mrs Thomas, who deserves a section to herself. But I am afraid I have not the literary ability to do justice to the subject. It needs a Kipling or John Buchan.

The first I knew of her would be in the early-ish nineties on Sundays, at the forenoon service. We would have all settled down for the service to begin: old Reverend James Robertson in the pulpit had just given out the first Psalm, when there would be a rustling and rush at the door leading to our side of the church, and a hurried procession of three girls and three boys, clattering in with tackety boots to a seat well in front and to the right – followed by Mr and Mrs Thomas, herding in their flock. A slow smile would pass over our faces, and Mr Robertson, with a twinkle in his eyes would pause, looking down at the procession over his spectacles. The only name I remember of the girls is Hetty, the middle one who was not strong – cardiac – and often in my hands: then Johnny, Willie and Charlie the boys. John was a solid, sensible, douce chap – very steady – and became something legal.

Willie was a queer, contrary lad, who went in for unusual pursuits, finally becoming an expert in the Zulu and Bantu languages, and being on the staff of the Censor in the Great War. I fancy he now has some University post in Canada.

Mr Thomas was a tailor and everything about him betokened it. They were all under middle height and he had a funny wee face with small but bushy side whiskers: long frock coat, well-brushed top hat on Sundays – but Mrs Thomas wore the breeks, and rules her family with a rod of iron. She was the 7th child of a 7th child and was highland and certainly had the uncanny 'second sight'. When a girl in Edinburgh, she told me, she could communicate at will with her uncle who lived at Haddington; and the two pretty well knew what each was doing. She was a little woman, in the late 30s when I first met her, with rosy complexion, bright, eager, glancing, black or mainly black eyes, black curly hair and always exuding animation.

She had wide hips for her size, and for Sunday wore voluminous skirts down to the feet no doubt bunched out with several petticoats; then her shoulders covered with a sort of cape or dolman, or in winter some kind of furry coat. She had a sharp tongue with which she did not spare her eldest and third daughters. The latter was a bit of a 'flee awa'', rather inclined to artificial aids to figure and complexion, such as were then in vogue.

122

They lived in a flat in Lochrin Buildings, beside Bruntsfield Links and later somewhere in Tollcross.

They had a set of the 'Gentleman's Magazine' of about the middle of the last century; and in one of these I was intrigued to find a tale pretty well foretelling the wireless. The story went that two gentlemen possessed two parts of a wonderful stone. One of them went to Africa, but when he wished to communicate with his friend at home at certain times arranged by them, he retired into his sanctum, took out the stone and by moving a pointer to different marks or letters talked with his friend.

Well, I had several curious experiences with the family: one of the most astonishing being when I was attending Charlie, the youngest, for influenza with inflammation of both lungs. He was very seriously ill, and one forenoon I had paid my usual visit and done what I could for the boy. In the early afternoon I decided to walk across to Minto Street to visit my great friend Dr Wm Hutton whom I've mentioned as one of my chums. I was then in 71 Leamington Terrace Just opposite Viewforth UP Church, now Bruntsfield Church, which stands as the corner of Leamington Terrace and Westhall Gardens.

I walked up the Terrace and across on to the road through the Links. I had not gone many yards on this road when a most intense feeling came over me that I ought to go and see Charlie. I argued with myself that I had seen him only an hour or two before, and walked on, but a second and a third time the influence passed on me; and, unable to resist it, I turned and went right down to Tollcross where the Thomas family lived then, and to my dismay found Charlie practically moribund. I got a bath of hot water, bags of hot salt with various stimulants. I worked away for an hour and then felt it was useless to go on as I was getting no reaction. But Mrs Thomas said, 'It's a richt, doctor, juist gae on he'll come round a'richt.' And after another hour's back breaking and exhausting work I got him rallied and in due time he made a pretty fair recovery.

After I got Charlie back to bed and safe for the present I asked Mrs Thomas why it was she was so sure Charlie would rally. 'Well, it's this way, doctor. After the three girls and Johnny I had another daughter who was the delight of my heart and the apple of my eye and I fair doted on her. But she took ill and died. I felt it sore, and was rebellious against Providence for allowing it, and day and night it was with me as a heavy burden, interfering with my work and my whole life. It was misery. Then one night I seemed to hear a voice upbraiding me for my rebellion against God's will and bidding me be resigned and more cheerful for the sake of my family; further, saying that in place of her I had lost I should have two boys who would be the comfort and support of my old life. So Willie and then Charlie came years after my last girl and how could they be the comfort of my old age if they were to be taken now, and me not an old woman yet, by a long way.'

Poor thing, Charlie died 2 or 3 years later: he never was strong: and she died in her 40s from cancer of the womb.

There was another incident connected with her, but this time an amusing one.

Hetty had been very ill and though far from strong she had come to a post-communion service one Sunday. The preacher was the minister of the old Dalry Road UP Church, and he had a fair bassoon of a booming voice. His subject, of all things, was the Judgement day. Moreover, he had a terrific burr and couldn't pronounce his r's: they sounded like 'aaghs' and he spoke very slowly and deliberately.

I was an elder then and was sitting just under him in the elder's seats so got the full blast. As he went on I got more and more restive and finally raging mad and angry, that a delicate girl like Hetty should be exposed to the storm.

'And the books were opened, and all was revealed. Have you ever seen a noble tree cut down, and looked at the concentric rings on the cut surface of the trunk? There are narrow rings and wide rings, the former made in years when there was no rain, when the heavens above were as brass, and drought was on the face of the whole earth. Then the wider rings: these point to years when the windows of heaven were opened, and the gentle rain fell on the earth beneath giving fertility and active growth and plentiful supplies meaning happiness for man and beast. "And all shall be revealed." A lady of my acquaintance was travelling by night from Holyhead to Dublin, and she lost her "umbaghella" and though she sought high and low throughout the ship she failed to find her "umbaghella". But one of Her Majesty's ships of war came near and cast the light of her search-light on the vessel, lighting it up from Stem to stern and the lady saw her umbaghella in the arms of a sailough (sailor) and she recognised her umbaghella, because her (at loudest) NAME was ENGRAVED in INEETIALS on the handle thereof.'

Well, Hetty had to be taken out to the session room by her mother and I followed at once, not waiting for the conclusion of the service. I found her lying on a sofa, recovering slowly and I paced up and down across the room, raging and raving at the rant and noise. I noticed Mrs Thomas's face began gradually to brighten up, as she saw the humour of the situation and she remarked quietly, 'Hey, doctor, shall I whistle up a tune?' This was to my dancing up and down. Of course the only thing to do was to laugh it off.

This recalls another funny incident which occurred at Newtongrange near Dalkeith when I was assistant to Dr Spalding of Gorebridge. I was rather a favourite in that mining community and when I wasn't pressed for time I used to sit down for a chat. One tall old miner I liked had for his chief reading the former illustrated weekly 'Ally Sloper' with loads of pretty girls showing their beauties freely. Well, he got in the talk one day. Hutton was then house-surgeon to John Chiene who was a great friend of Spaldings (who came from Maryland, USA) and Hutton had been looking after the practice for a bit and went about with a somewhat swelled head. They called him 'The Professor'. 'You know, doctor, we like you but we don't like those big wigs and professors who can tell all that is going on inside you and all that's wrong with you. We prefer ordinary, not so clever folk to attend us, who know us and are kind to us, and sympathise with and know our ways. Just like yourself, doctor.' I laughed – the double-edged nature of the compliment was delightful.

This man with his 4 or 5 sons, during the great mining strikes of about 1874, had brought into the house between them about £75 a week: and they saved it. He told me of a friend who had gone into a hotel in Edinburgh with his pockets full of money and heard a gentleman asking a waiter for a bootjack – to lever off his boots from the heel. This man, half tipsy, called another waiter and to be more than level with the gent ordered two bootjacks. He thought it was a kind of drink.

(End of letter.)

28th August 1940

Dr Bruce was very good to me, and your mother was quite a favourite of his. When a student she was clerk on a heart case and made such a good job of it that it was held up as an example for the others.

There were curious sounds or murmurs originating from the mitral valve – that between the upper and lower chambers on the right side of the heart. Usually one blowing sound is heard caused by the blood rushing through a narrowed opening or through one with rough surfaces – both due to disease. Occasionally there are two or exceptionally three murmurs, due to the to and fro movement of the blood across the surfaces. But your mother maintained that she had heard four distinct sounds. Bruce at first wouldn't believe it: but after careful examination and listening he had to admit that she was right. I think this was after she was engaged and was wearing that lovely emerald and diamond ring I gave her: and of course I was assisting Bruce at Surgeon's Hall so that things all round were very friendly.

After we came back from our honeymoon near Fecamp and Oulton Broad, Bruce gave a dinner party in our honour at his house in Moray Place, and of course took in your mother who sat at his right side as the principal guest. She wore her wedding dress, made out of white silk brocade with valuable Brussels lace about the neck and corsage. There is sure to be some bits of the lovely figures – flowers etc. – material and certainly the Brussels Lace in the big tin box with her other dainty and valuable things. The dresses at that time were full skirted and came down to the ankles – very graceful and becoming on one who could carry them. *(Parts of the dress have been donated to the Norwich Castle Museum, with some other clothes of Minnie Shennan's.)*

I remember well one occasion during our engagement when she donned for the first time a beautiful softly grey check tailor made costume and we walked from her digs in Forrest Road along

127

College St. to Nicolson Street for the train to take us to Newington – to 95 Mayfield Road. Going swiftly along College Street, we passed some cheeky little girls who were greatly struck with your mother's appearance and called out, 'Oh, Chase me girls!!' to our great amusement. I kept that up for a long time.

She had another lovely flowing dress of pale mauve gauze or net, over a blue silk underskirt; but I always liked a royal blue dress she had on when I proposed to her in the old Surgeon's Museum. It was of soft, gauzy woolly stuff and suited her down to the ground as all her things did. This was worn with a fairly large hat, with a large white feather pom-pom. I took several snaps of her in this dress, one at Cromer on a visit there in which she looks fine.

But I must not let memory make me wander – though it often does.

Another of Bruce's and Bramwell's and Gibson's contemporaries has just passed away at 89: Dr Wm Russell, who was pathologist to the Edinburgh Royal Infirmary along with Simms Woodhead when I was a student. When 51 or 52 he married Beatrice Ritchie, a tall very handsome and graceful black-haired student of a crowd a year or so before your mother. She had two sons and three daughters, four of them becoming doctors. One of the daughters married a Russian. She must have married after we did. They were always good friends and I admired Mrs Russell greatly, she developed that curious type of personality that can only be called

128

'graciousness'. Mrs Kitywalk had something of it. All these women loved your mother dearly, like everyone – man or woman – who came in contact with her.

Dr Russell taught pathology and late Clinical Medicine to the women students for years. I had some of them also for practical work. It was a happy, busy time.

Byrom Bramwell was a very able physician with a gift for getting things done. He came from Newcastle and his folks had been in lucrative business so Byrom was well off, quite apart from his own consulting practice which was very extensive. We may have attended all the Professors in their wards but we never missed Bramwell's out-patient clinics. He would bring in a patient and work out the case by question and answer bringing up student after student to take part, often unimportant, but all leading up to the concluding diagnosis. It was all taken down word for word by a shorthand clerk and BB published many of these cases with the dialogue in a monthly or bi-monthly 'Clinical Record' all of which he put together himself. I have 7 or 8 of them which contain cases for which I furnished the post-mortem or pathological report.

Sometimes he would fumble in his pocket for a small tape measure and sometimes it would come out rusty. 'Ah, gentlemen, fishing,' and then he would digress on how to tell the weight of a fish by measuring its girth – so many inches in girth – so many pounds or ounces weight. I believe it works out very nearly correct.

He was tall but rather round shouldered, with a biggish head and prominent roman nose. He spoke with a slight nasal tone and was given to putting an 'R' at the end of a word ending in 'a'. 'The idear' for example. 'Meningitis chronicar interar haemorrhagicar.' Both he and Russell were President of the Royal College of Physicians in their time: and a few years ago Edwin Bramwell, the son, was President, looking in his late 50s or perhaps later ridiculously like his father. He comes or came regularly for fishing to the hotel at Bridge of Alford, where in the dining room hangs his photo.

Byrom was knighted late in life. I think his great disappointment was failing to secure the Chair of Medicine after Grainger Stewart died. His testimonials and letter of appreciation make a hefty book of about 100 pages. Perhaps he overdid the printing.

(The famous case of your mother's *(her death in 1932?)* is preserved entire somewhere in amongst her papers. Perhaps in the big box.)

(End of letter.)

When I graduated in July 1890, the problem was what to do. I was not offered a resident post in the Infirmary and doubt if I would have afforded to accept one, as there was not much free cash about. Professor Chiene offered me a surgeon's job on a transport conveying coolies to and from East Africa: but it was to be a 2 year job so I turned it down as I had to begin to earn my keep.

I forget who recommended it, but in September or October I went to Broxburn as assistant to Dr Freeland. I had been doing locums in August. In fact I saw my first patients in general practice in the afternoon or evening of the day I graduated. Both were young women: one for a tooth extraction. I got most of it out – the first I had attempted. (I remember the appearance of that tooth still.) We had had no instruction in dentistry, such as they all get now.

The second complained of gastric trouble and as I had been taught I went over all the systems including her nervous system and was still unable to make a diagnosis. I went next door to a friendly doctor and described what I had made out. 'Oh! Just indigestion,' wanting a little dilute nitro-hydrochloric acid and a bitter infusion along with it. It was a good lesson, to expect simple ordinary things, and not out of the way conditions which after all are not at all common.

I soon learned that the bulk of practice consists in little things: and that one's patients are mostly women and children. I remember one man who came to ask how to cohabit safely, that is for himself. I was not very sympathetic, telling him that after all it was not really necessary for a man to have women promiscuously all the time. He left me in a bad temper, thinking I was a poor sort of doctor, as his opinion was the directly opposite, and the man whose practice I was taking was very easy on such things. (Dr Hamilton Wylie, George Place, Leith Walk.) Millard was the rather decent chap next door.

Wylie used to shock me with his remarks about Christ: and at last I kicked at it and told him what I thought. He took it quite nicely and kept off such subjects: though he did tell me I should have made a success as a parson, as I 'would have attracted the women' and so had a good time. What an extraordinary idea of a parson's work! We kept quite good friends until his death from blocking of the blood vessels of the lungs, and he told me to be sure I got one of his pictures; he had quite a good collection – and the evening after he died I took a taxi and brought home that painting of the neighbourhood of Musselburgh which hangs over the fireplace in the back room. It was my first good picture.

At intervals for 8 to 10 years I used to help Wylie occasionally with his practice, or take charge of it when he was on holiday: and once late at night he asked me to help him in clearing out an early miscarriage from a woman's womb. He seemed unusually nervous, and in the end I had to take the instrument and complete the operation satisfactorily. All apparently went well but I was rather surprised when he sent me £3/3/- (3 guineas) for my help.

Years after, when in practice on my own account I was asked to attend a married woman in Murrayfield in one of those flats just at the s-shaped bend looking on to the Water of Leith near the road bridge spanning it. After a visit or two she said, 'You don't remember me, doctor?' 'No, I can't say I do.' 'Well, do you remember coming to a house off Minto Street to help in delivering an abortion with Dr Wylie.' 'Yes, I remember it well.' 'Didn't Dr Wylie tell you about it?' 'No, nothing beyond the operation!' 'Well, I was housekeeper to the gentleman of the house and I became in the family way to him, and he persuaded Dr Wylie, for a high fee, to bring on abortion.' 'This is the first I've heard of that,' said I quite horrified; because if it had got out I should have been very severely dealt with, probably imprisoned and should have lost my degree and not been able to practice in any way.

It was a dirty trick to play on an unsuspecting friend. Of course it was criminal and quite illegal. I was very careful never to examine any young woman without someone else in the room. Many are wily enough to take advantage of a young doctor. Several times I have been asked to induce abortion and I expect most young doctors have been tempted in that way: but it was always the shortest way to the door that was shown to such folk.

Well, I went to Broxburn and was there for 9 or 10 months, £6 a month and my board. No-one, even a woman doctor, would look at an assistantship now under £300 a year: and they get it, and in place of the 2 or 3 guineas a week as locum we got in those days, 8 and 10 guineas are asked and got all right even by young newly fledged chaps.

I quite enjoyed that time. It was heavy work. Some days I had 100 visits to pay – during epidemics of scarlet fever or influenza or diphtheria; but it was a case of 5 minutes in a house, then out to the next up the rows of miner's houses. It is very extraordinary that I used to have cases of scarlet fever – children – in the same box bed with newly delivered women; but we never had an infection from child to woman though the risk is now regarded as extremely serious.

The two diphtheria epidemics I worked through were the most trying. It was before the days of protective inoculation and curative serum which was introduced in 1894 or 95, and one passed from case to case trying tracheotomy, inserting a tube in the windpipe and other things – always or almost always without success and it was awful to watch the poor kids struggling for breath, getting more and more blue in the face, knowing that one could not save them. Most of them died.

The influenza was then of what was termed a sthenic type (or strong) and the men could stand vigorous treatment. We used to give them a very strong purgative which kept them emptying their bowels all night. In the mornings they were very much better though feeling very weak and in a day or two they were back at work. Such treatment would kill patients nowadays. But I was a damned fool. One day I saw an old lady about late 60s or 70, and gave her the same treatment. Next morning all she said to me reproachfully was, 'Man, doctor, were ye no feared?' What a fool I felt. I wasn't asked back to that house.

I delivered over 100 women there without a single accident and without losing a mother: though I lost two kiddies who were feet first. We had no antiseptics, just thorough cleansing with hot soapy water: and I learned to put a midwifery forceps on to the head of the child to assist delivery by propulsion almost without the woman knowing it and almost always without anaesthetic. They were a hardy lot. The only two women we lost had been attended at their confinements by midwives, dirty-handed slatterns, and in spite of all we could do, they died of sepsis.

I had one very nasty experience there. One bitter frosty winter night when sitting with Freeland talking we heard a great row in the street outside the gate. I went out and found a young woman maniacal. Freeland told me to take her home and give her 1/2 a grain of morphine. I did so, and next morning she was dead – not so long after I had taken her home. There was a great upset for I was blamed for causing her death from overdose of morphine. No doubt the exposure had something to do with it; but in any case 1/2 a grain is a fairly big dose. It would have sufficed in an ordinary case.

Well, Sir Henry Littlejohn came out and did a post-mortem. He found the membranes of the brain very congested and reported that that was result of the mania: that the morphia had nothing to do with it; clearing me completely to the satisfaction of all concerned. But the trouble and snag was and still is to my own mind viz that similar appearances can be caused by overdoses of morphine and I have never been able to clear the morphia of blame.

But Littlejohn always took the line to protect a fellow medical even though a new graduate. He was a good friend for many years after until his death well on in the seventies. He was a little chap and active as mercury jumping on and off from cars in motion to the end not allowing conductors to stop for him.

134

Littlejohn was Medical Officer of Health for Edinburgh and also Lecturer on Medical Jurisprudence at Surgeons' Hall. His opposite number at the Varsity was Sir Douglas Maclagan, who had a brother, Archbishop of York, and who as a young man, and his father before him, attended Mother when a young woman.

Littlejohn's lectures were chiefly made up of stories, some of them pretty broad: and I thought I could be better at the Varsity; but I think I should have had a great stock of his stories had I continued to attend his lectures. I went only to the first.

I urged one of his class assistants who was later Sir Andrew Balfour, head of the Tropical school in London, and Littlejohn's son Harvey who succeeded him both at Surgeons' Hall and Varsity to put as many of these on record as they could remember but unfortunately it was never done and the Edinburgh world is all the poorer. They were all about his cases, doubtless well embroidered. He was a past master of embroidery of tales.

He was Editor of the Edinburgh Medical Journal for many years in addition to many other activities.

Once he went round the Museum of the Royal College of Surgeons with me and pointed out the coal-miner' lung, impregnated with coal dust – from which the condition was first described by two Edinburgh doctors – the famous Gregory and the equally famous and handsome Christian who preceded Maclagan in his chair. The other half-lung is in the University Museum. I give this full credit in my book. It was not fully recognised until re-discovered in Germany, years later.

A year or two before he died, he was presented with his portrait and it is a most characteristic likeness. It hangs in the Royal College of Surgeons.

I was talking to the Officer – Cresswell – a day or two after the presentation and was greatly amused by Cresswell's account of a conversation with Sir Henry after the presentation. 'I've just come up to see where you're going to put my portrait, Cresswell.' Cresswell, who was a bit of a wag, said, 'Oh! Sir Henry, you may depend on me putting you in a nice warm place.' 'I know what you mean, you divvil, Cresswell, I know what you mean.'

There was no lawyer the match for Sir Henry [Littlejohn] when the latter was in the witness box. In Parliament House, it used to be (pos?) 'Witness'; (comparative) 'Skilled witness'; (superlative) 'Sir Henry Littlejohn'; and sometimes 'Liar'; 'Damned Liar'; 'Sir Henry Littlejohn' as pos (?), comparative and superlative.

He was one of the kindest-hearted men going but did his damndest for his own side.

In one famous case – I can't go further – both he and McLagan came a cropper, almost the only experience of that kind he had. He was asked the reaction of milk and for the life of him couldn't recall it. Coming out he met McLagan going into the box. He whispered, 'For goodness sake, watch out for milk.' Rather extraordinary such a simple thing to floor two such experienced and eminent experts.

He took Harvey out to his cases, ever the nastiest, when the latter was still in his early teens; and naturally he followed in his footsteps, but though quite good and well informed, Harvey never approached the personality and force of his father.

Of course the great value of Sir Henry's lectures was in the stories which fixed details of cases and circumstances in a way not approachable by purely didactic lecturing: and it was a mistake on my part jibbing at them and not absorbing them all with the lessons they taught. But I could talk about these great Edinburgh personalities, that I knew so well, for hours.

But to return to Broxburn. The chief thing that diminished the value of that year to me was that Freeland and I took days about to visit the patients thus relieving me of all or almost all responsibility. Now that, as you will know, was a mistake. To get the best out of a job you must have responsibility. The result was that I got rather careless and was not sorry when the engagement came to an end.

He was a Glasgow graduate and like most Glasgow men had a chemist's shop with a consulting room at the back in which we saw most of our patients who were not confined to the house. I must say we shoved them through very quickly. It was a case of a few pence a week from each workman and I fancy that included attendance on the family as well. I doubt if F. would make more than £800 or £1000 a year: but that was a good income in those days. There was nothing heavy to keep up, the heaviest a pony (cob) and small light dog-cart – very easy to drive and on foggy days or nights on country roads, when one could not see the sides of the road, one just let the reins lie loose on the pony's back and she kept the centre of the road all the way – not much traffic, almost none at night and of course no mechanical traction except road engines and no motors.

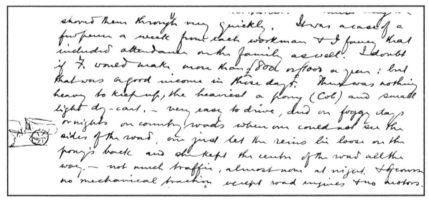

There was a large Irish element in the population all congregated to the west of the village across the bridge over the works railway. I got on well with them and liked them very much: and they often got in the way of sending for me before sending for the priest. It's usually the other way about in serious illness in Roman Catholics.

The one I remember best was a great fat woman about 20 stone weight whom I used to meet all over the place – and frequently at confinements of her daughters or daughters-in-law. She was an excellent manager and quite good assistant never getting flurried. One night when I had washed my hands and was drying them before the fire, meantime chatting away to this woman. – when she suddenly made a grab at my collar, a rather startling action. Then she said, 'Well, dochtor, they till me I canna catch them things, unless I fling meself down on top of them.' It was a flea that had transferred from a bed to the white of my collar.

Occasionally she was in a serious mood, as when she told me she had a son training for the priesthood in the Scots College in Paris, and had to save up to meet his expenses, adding plaintively, 'Dochtor, I wonder if it will all be put to my credit in the hereafter.' Of course she meant her passage through purgatory and I assured her that I was quite certain it all would be put to her credit – which rather comforted her. These Irish are a mixture of the clever and rather wily adult of experience and the childlike and simple. That's what makes them so attractive, though they can be so exasperating.

Freeland and his wife – they had no children – belonged to the New Jerusalem Church i.e. they were Swedenborgians, believing that after death folk live much as here, in similar surroundings though unseen by us and all around us. She was a little hard-faced stodgy woman, sterile of ideas as of children.

He was a decent chap, red-haired, rather barrel-chested and with a constant cough, which I fancy was not always or wholly caused by smoking. He smoked a tobacco which was made up into tiny blocks or coarse granules, which I haven't seen since. His wife had two very weedy brothers who visited frequently; they seemed to me to be boastful wasters as well as badly developed weeds. Freeland's great friend was the Manager of the Oil Works. I forget his name.

The work's manager often came in in the evening; his house was next door to the Firs, as Freeland's house was named. Once when he was in, one of these little weeds was boasting as usual, and saying that when they were out with their father they sometimes had beer to their supper. He thought this a tremendous statement but the manager promptly pricked the bubble by remarking very acidly, 'Well, ma mannie, that would make you wet your bed that night.' A regular guffaw flattened out the young man.

I used frequently to visit Willie Brand, a grocer who came from Bathgate and set up business in Broxburn. He married one of the Dougals, as I mentioned in 'The Orator Looks Back'. I saw that one of his sons evidently in some important position about Broxburn died a month or two ago.

This was all at a time when Broxburn Oil Co was at the height of its success, its shares round about £2 and paying good dividends – before the discovery of oil-wells in the States. That messed up the shale oil producers, though they are recovering now, and making a good thing of cracking oil – petrol – and of various by-products.

My chief friends were William Forbes, the assistant to Reverend Ian Primrose of the UP Church, that one at the east end of the town, and John Clark the underground manager. They were bachelors in those days though later they married sisters – daughters of the tenant of that farm (Law) still seen between the road east of Broxburn and the big spent shale being to the north.

They were great chaps, full of fun and always ready for a prank, usually some practical joke played on mutual friends. We dubbed ourselves the 'Three Graces'. Forbes was Faith, Clark was Charity and I was Hope. We were not quite satisfied with this distribution till either Forbes or I remembered that the Latin for Hope was Spes and that made all correct – so it was Fides, Caritas and Spes. And we had our symbols: mine was the Anchor of Hope and the other two had the cross and the shield. I forget now which but I think Forbes had the cross. So well recognised and almost notorious did our pranks become that some of our friends dubbed us the three dis-graces and tales of our doings still survive.

I forget a lot of them now but the most notable was an April-fools' day one: when we sent notes to the Manager of the Works, the (... .?) minister and the 'Bishop' as Forbes called Primrose, to call that night at some unusual destination. They were all caught out, but very much amused nevertheless.

It was a Wednesday night and Forbes was with Primrose in the mid-week prayer meeting, when the latter announced that he had been summoned to a very important meeting and would have to leave Forbes to close the prayer meeting. Of course Forbes was a victim of suppressed giggles, but as he said later, he just managed to 'pit up a petition' before joining the other two of us who were waiting outside and had watched Primrose hurrying away on his wild goose chase. As a matter of fact it did good, as these men when they met got on to talk and came to a harmonious settlement of some matters that had been troubling them.

It was extraordinary how the time passed. The manager of the Uphall Oil Company was an Englishman, Bagshaw, and he had a nice wife and a daughter Ada who was a bit soft and sentimental. She had been at school at Bathgate and my sisters had known her – a bit older than I was. We used often to go there for tennis. I remember once smashing the ball from the back of the court, right between Ada's shoulders – she happened to be my partner that game and though it must have hurt some – only a thin blouse covering the skin, she made out it was nothing, though my apologies would not prevent her thinking some.

Sometimes I went up with her to the old church up the hill, I believe a bit ancient – and played the pipe organ, while she blew it. I rather enjoyed that.

I don't recall which of us, I believe it was myself, remembered how to make a cock-crow – out of a cocoa-tin and a long piece of waxed string through a hole in the bottom of the tin. Dragging the fingers for a longer or shorter distance along the string produces a noise remarkably like a cock's crow. One night Clark and I were in the

Bagshaw's house, when we remarked late at night, a cock crowing first at the garden wall, then at the steps at the front door. The Bagshaws were greatly puzzled: and Forbes coming in a little later could do little (or would) to elucidate the extraordinary phenomenon. I fancy Mr Bagshaw had his suspicions though being a sportsman he did not give us away.

There were no motors, no cinemas or theatres, in fact no public amusements in the place and yet we never wearied.

Freeland had a small greenhouse – still there – built on to the east gable of his house and warmed from the house. He had a big geranium up the wall on one side of the communicating door and an equally large heliotrope on the other. He was keen on primulas too and had quite a number of both large and small flowering types. I drew some of these in colour in my sketch book on slack occasions.

I used to have chats with the Irish Priest too. He seemed a decent sort of cove and I got on all right with him. I was interested in his unruly flock too. The winter was not very severe as a whole so far as I remember, though one night I had to drive to Winchburgh over ice-covered roads and there was some camber in those days.

We were never invited to the works to see the processes, though I dare say we could have gone all over them had we wanted; but at that time I was not so interested in manufacturing processes as I became later.

Clark died 6 or 7 years ago. He had been up in Aberdeen a few months before and had missed me at Marischal: but I wrote and fixed up a visit to his home to talk over old times: but it never came.

You know about Forbes, still in his first charge, and his relations in Aberdeen have heard a lot about the Graces. One of them, a bonny girl, was in my class and I expect hardly harmonised the tales with her gruff professor.

Ends (Page 138.)

Acknowledgements

David Shennan passed the original letter(s) to Chris some time in the late 1980s as part of his 'Shennan Archive'. Almost all the rest of that archive has been deposited at the Norfolk Record Office in Norwich (material that related to David's mother, Minnie Green, and her family) or at the archive of the University of Aberdeen (material that related to David's father, Theodore).

The original handwritten letter was first typed up by Chris' wife, Miranda, in the early 1990s. At some point, it was also typed up by Jean Shennan, Theodore's daughter, who was born in 1936. After Jean's death in September 2021, Chris edited those two versions alongside the original text to produce this final document.

Essentially all the script is as written by Theodore to David. Some limited editing has taken place to improve the layout and punctuation, and also to introduce greater consistency between variants of the same word (e.g. professor, Professor, Prof, Prof. and Street, St, St. etc).

A number of the illustrations are taken straight from the letter (Theodore was highly competent at drawing and painting). The portraits are copies of ones that Chris has – most of the photographic archive has gone to Norwich and Aberdeen, as mentioned above.